DARK NIGHTS IN THE CASTLE OF THE PRINCE

Memoirs of a Cuban university student who served as a paratrooper in Brigade 2506, the Bay of Pigs, as a political prisoner in the Castle of the Prince, and his freedom and long and successful exile in the United States.

CUBA Y SUS JUECES COLLECTION

EDICIONES UNIVERSAL, Miami, Florida, 2021

ALBERTO J. BOLET

DARK NIGHTS IN THE CASTLE OF THE PRINCE

Memoirs of a Cuban university student who served as a paratrooper in Brigade 2506, the Bay of Pigs, as a political prisoner in the Castle of the Prince, and his freedom and long and successful exile in the United States.

Copyright © 2021 by Alberto J. Bolet

First edition, 2021

EDICIONES UNIVERSAL
P.O. Box 450353 (Shenandoah Station)
Miami, FL 33245-0353. USA
(Since 1965)

E-mail: ediciones@ediciones.com
http://www.ediciones.com

Library of Congress Catalog Card No.: 2021944181
ISBN: 978-1-59388-322-5

Text preparation: María Cristina Zarraluqui

Cover design: Luis García Fresquet

Cover photos: Paratrooper training in Quetzaltenango base, Guatemala during 1961. First Battalion's uniform shoulder patch.

Back Cover photo: The author attending the 60th anniversary of the Bay of Pigs Invasion at the former Opa Locka Air Base in 2021. He is standing in front of one of the B-26 aircraft that participated in the invasion.

All rights are reserved.
No part of this book may be reproduced or
transmitted in any form or by any means, electronic
or mechanical, including photocopying machines, tape recorders
or computerized systems, without the written permission
of the author, except in the case of brief quotations
embodied in critical articles or in magazines.
For more information:
ediciones@ediciones.com

This book is dedicated to the love of my life, my wife Margarita Celorio Bolet, who has walked with me through good times and bad, who never complains and always helps, who never asks but always gives freely; to me and all that are in need.

Peachtree Corners, 2021

TABLE OF CONTENTS

INTRODUCTION 13

CUBA 1940'S – 1950'S 15
    Respect for the Natural Environment 19
    The Role of Music in Cuban Society 20
        El Carnaval de la Habana 23
        La Playa de Varadero 26
    El Colegio de La Salle 27
        Lessons in Cuban History I Learned in School 30
    Summers in the US 32

LA REVOLUCIÓN 35
    Fidel Castro and the 26th of July Movement 35
        Fidel's Youth 35
    Insights Into the Truth about the Cuban Revolution 39
    Cuba's Descent Into Tyranny 42
        Armas Para Que? 42
        The Destruction of the Cuban Economy 44
        Why Socialism Never Works 44
        Reign of Terror 51
    My Brother and I Leave Cuba for the First Time 53

LIFE IN MIAMI 1959-1960 55
    The CIA and the Miami Cuban Exile Community
    in 1959-1960 56
    US Policy Actions Related to Cuba 1959-60 59
        The Dulles Brothers 60
        Dick Bissell and the Cuba Special Group 62
        CIA Cuba Group Strategies 64

Kennedy Administration Relationship with Cuban Exiles...65
Recruiting Brigade Members in the US 66

EL ESCAMBRAY 71

Raúl Celorio's Story 72
 The Revolution Comes to Sancti Spiritus.........................76
 Leaving Home 78
Los Bandidos del Escambray 79
 Raulito's Story 81
 Fighting in the Escambray 82
The Girls Leave Cuba 83
Escambray Epilogue 84

GUATEMALA 85

Paratroopers 87

NICARAGUA 91

Air Operations – April 15 1961 92
 April 15 Air Strikes 93
 April 16..95
Paratroopers in Puerto Cabezas – Happy Valley Airbase –
April 15-16 97

INVASION 99

Monday 100
 Air Operations – Monday April 17................................103
Tuesday...106
 Air Operations – Tuesday April 18 110
Wednesday..111
 Air Operations – Wednesday April 19 113
The Celia...114
La Cienaga..115

La Rastra 118
    Facts As Outlined in Human Rights Abuse Lawsuits 119
    La Rastra Murders - A Witness' Story 121

PRISON 125
  El Palacio de los Deportes 125
  El Hospital Naval 127
  El Castillo del Príncipe 128
    Prison Life 129
    The Tractors for Prisoners Committee 130
    The Great Escape 131
    The Trial 133
    El Juicio de la Brigada – William D Muir 134
    In the Lion's Den 135
    The Charanga Band 136
    The Missile Crisis 136
    Christmas 1962 137
    Flying Home 138
  Happy Ending - Life in the States 140
    Special Friends 141

APPENDICES 145
  Appendix 1 145
  Table 2. Brief Timeline of Cuban History (1492 to 1958) 145
    A. Spanish Colonial Period – 1492 to 1898 146
    B. US Intervention – 1898 to 1902 147
    C. First Cuban Republic – 1902 to 1958 148
  Policy Failures – Cuba Project 150
  Foreign Policy Impacts 151
  Table 3 - Consequences of the Failure to Depose
    Castro in 1961 151

Naval Units Involved In Bay of Pigs Invasion 156
    US Navy Ships Deployed to "Escort" Bay of Pigs Invasion Ships 156
    US Navy Ships Assigned to Directly Support Invasion Forces 158
Colonel Juan R López de la Cruz Fight for Human Rights 160
Letter to the European Court of Human Rights from the Committee to Assist Dissidents – Brigade 2506 162
My Prayer 164
Appendix 2: Digital Images and Tables 166

BIBLIOGRAPHY 173

INTRODUCTION

I started to write this book as a gift to my children and grandchildren. I very seldom spoke to them about my experiences as a teenager related to coming to this country and my service in the Cuban Brigade sent by the CIA to defeat the Castro Government.

In the search for veracity and confirmation of my recollections of events, I spoke to many people who were involved in these events, some in my family, or members of my wife's family, some in the Brigade. I have documented their stories as accurately to their own recollections as possible.

This book consists of many components: it is a reflection of my own and my family's personal life experiences; it is an analysis of the decisions that led to many of the key events that shaped my life; and most importantly, it is a cry of warning to the citizens of my beloved adopted country, the United States of America, to avoid the mistake of electing politicians who would replace American freedoms with socialist inspired policies and institutions.

My personal experiences in this book are a faithful recollection of events. All names are real names or aliases used by the individuals at the time. I am personally responsible for the veracity of my analysis and for my interpretation of motives and consequences.

My character was formed in large part, because I participated in an effort to overthrow the government of the Cuban dictator Fidel Castro. I hope my experiences can be of use to those that read this book.

Image 1: *Castillo del Príncipe*

Alberto J Bolet
Assault Brigade 2506
1 Bon Airborne
Co. C

CUBA 1940'S – 1950'S

If reincarnation is real, I must have been a saint in my prior life. Destiny decided that I would be born on the Island of Cuba in the nineteen forties. I lived in a place that was as close to paradise as you could get.

Image 2: *My Brother Armando and I*

My first memories as a child are rooted in our neighborhood, Miramar. It was a playground for the children who grew up there.

My brother Armando and I rode our bikes through its tree-lined streets in complete freedom. Miramar was an affluent area of La Habana, but our family was not considered upper class. As a matter of fact, my father was a musician, and I was born in a duplex. My family enjoyed a lifestyle which was not solely based on our family's wealth. We enjoyed living on an island with a rich culture and with amazing natural beauty. My brother and I were surrounded by family and friends. However, my life changed drastically at age 5 when my mother divorced my father. My mother eventually remarried a wonderful man.

Image 3: *Aeropuerto de Rancho Boyeros*
The author in the middle, my brother Armando with the cowboy hat and our neighbor and great friend Reynaldo Fernandez Mendoza at the Rancho Boyeros Airport expansion job

My stepfather, Arístides López-Calleja, was a civil engineer and had a construction business. His company completed many projects: the most important of these included the expansion of the runway at Rancho Boyeros International Airport to accommodate jets, a segment of the Circuito Sur Expressway in Las Villas Province, the first pedestrian overpass in Avenida Carlos Tercero in La Habana, and many more. Because he had a habit of taking us along to his worksites, I had the opportunity to travel to all six of the original Cuban Provinces. Castro later changed the maps and added many others.

We belonged to the Club de Profesionales[1] which had two pools, a restaurant and bar, a tennis court, a squash court, and an ocean front location with a pier. There were a very large number of similar clubs with equal numbers of facilities in La Habana that entertained a large percentage of the entirety of the city's middle class population. It was four blocks from our house. Although there were many other clubs in the city with much nicer facilities and more restrictive admission requirements (i.e. Habana Yacht Club, Habana Biltmore, Country Club, Vedado Tennis, Miramar Yacht Club, etc.), as children we preferred our neighborhood club. Many of my school friends were members of the other fancier clubs, but we were perfectly happy with ours. I was able to get home from school, jump on my bike, and be in the ocean in fifteen minutes.

My brother and I preferred to be outside as much as possible, so we formed a "neighborhood gang" when we were very young (about 10). It was called "Los Halcones Negros" (the black hawks) after a DC comic book we all liked. We built forts in empty lots and pretended we were jet fighter pilots fighting the bad guys. Members of the gang included: José Ramón de la Torre, Miguel Ángel Junco, Reynaldo Fernández Mendoza, his sister Muñe, and my brother and I. We all lived a block away from each other and were really very close. We enjoyed an enviable freedom as children as the only house rules were to do well academically in school and to be home by 6:00 pm for dinner. Lack of parental micromanagement allowed me a different type of learning environment; one that honed the necessary social skills to develop and keep strong peer and professional relationships throughout my lifetime.

---

[1] Club for Professionals

My family did not belong to Cuba's upper class (there was an upper class in Cuba and admission to it was determined by birth or extreme wealth). There were a large number of Cuban families with similar backgrounds to mine who worked at regular jobs or had small businesses and who shared similar lifestyles (equivalent to US Middle Class). This had been true for most of the twentieth century as Cuban society matured in the shadow of the United States, which provided a blueprint not only for our constitutional republic, but also benefited from established, very strong, commercial ties with US corporations that provided easy access to western technological advances; yet Cuba was deeply rooted culturally in Europe, due to its centuries of Spanish colonial rule, and deeply rooted in the cultures and agrarian practices of countries in West Africa who gave us the Yoruba based culture, Santeria, love for music, and joy of life.

My stepfather lost his business in a court battle over a personal, nonprofessional matter, so he bought a farm in Cangrejeras, where we raised chickens to sell the eggs. We also had two dairy cows and a bull, the cows provided milk for our use; additionally, we sold the excess to local residents and small grocery stores. As a teenager, I learned to drive the panel truck we used to deliver eggs and milk to our clients.

I learned many valuable lessons in life from my stepfather: the value of hard work, entrepreneurship, but most of all, I learned to confront adversity and to have the necessary courage to overcome serious obstacles.

Two incidents shaped my character as a young man growing up in Cuba. We had a beautiful black Criollo stallion with a notoriously bad temper. My stepfather knew I was afraid of riding this horse, so one day he saddled the horse and told me to get on it. He then smacked the hind quarters of the horse which took off like a rocket. I had to manage to control the horse before he could throw me. I stopped him well short of the barbed wire fence that was in our way. My stepfather knew I could control the horse, but he helped me to overcome my own destructive fear in the process.

The second incident also involved a horse. I liked to ride a small mare we had bareback, with only the halter to control her. One day the horse and I were galloping on a dirt road and a snake crossed the road in front of us. The mare naturally was spooked by the snake, stopped suddenly, and reared on her hind legs. I did not let go of the reins, which caused me to slide down her back and pull her on top of me. I was extremely lucky not to break any bones, but I learned two hard lessons: If you ride a horse bareback, you better keep your eyes on the road, and you need to let go of the reins if she decides to throw you.

Our lives were very active.

One of my favorite childhood activities involved skin diving with my brother and friends – we used to jump into the ocean at the club or go on fishing trips with my stepfather. A childhood hero of mine was Jacques Costeau, a French naval officer turned conservationist and explorer. I used the same speargun and employed the same tactics I had learned while reading about Costeau's adventures. Using a snorkel and armed with an Arbalete speargun, we really enjoyed diving in about thirty meters of water looking for snappers, groupers, yellow tails, parrot fish, or anything that was edible. Spearfishing was fun, but I only speared fish I could eat. You had to be careful with the occasional encounters with barracudas and sharks. The marine life was spectacular, especially in the cayerías (a large number of small barrier islands surround Cuba's north and southern coasts). Fish of all colors and sizes, sponges, Caribbean lobsters, moray eels, and many other types of marine life were abundant and accessible to divers and fishermen. It was a wonderland for teens who loved the ocean.

Respect for the Natural Environment

I remember an incident that I liked to tell my kids as a cautionary tale when we went to the beach. I used to go spear fishing with a neighbor named Kiki Ardavin in a place called "Las bocas del Río

Salado"[2] east of the town of Santa Fe. There were two sharks that lived there eating whatever came out of the mouth of the river. I did not know at the time that sharks had a special sense that could detect very small traces of blood in the water and would follow a trail of blood back to its origin. As soon as we caught something, the sharks would show up and circle us. Every time we had to dump our catch and swim like hell back to the shore. I am sure those sharks loved us for providing them with many meals. The fish I managed to catch and keep were cooked and served immediately to our family.

From a very early age I learned to respect our natural environment when I saw what pollution does to reefs and to the environment that nurture fisheries. To this day I abhor pollution and polluters.

Later I found out that my future wife had a beach home in the town called Playa Habana, about five kilometers west of there. We never met until much later in the United States, but that is another story.

The Role of Music in Cuban Society

Music was pivotal in Cuban life. Cubans loved to sing, dance, and party. This cut across all economic and racial lines. Cubans loved "guajiras", which are Cuban "country music", played on all local radio stations, mixed with love songs, slow Cuban danzones, and music from Europe, the US, and South America.

Consider this fact: many prominent musicians from the United States, South America, and Europe came to La Habana during the forties and fifties to perform or to relax because of this stigma-free, music loving audience. A perfect example is Nat King Cole, probably one of the most iconic singers from the United States in

---

[2] Bocas... The mouth of the Salado River – where this river emptied to the ocean

the fifties. Cole recorded many records in Cuba in Spanish. He performed multiple times in the Cabaret Tropicana, one of the most beautiful venues in the world at that time. His records were in my home and played in the homes of every Cuban household that had teenagers.

Other examples are the long list of Cuban performing artists of all colors and backgrounds: famous examples of singers and musicians included Celia Cruz, Benny Moré, Dámaso Pérez Prado, Vicentico Váldes, among others. International and local performing acts like the Chavales de España, Orquesta Aragón, and El Trío Los Panchos performed regularly. These artists were immensely popular with Cuban teenagers and young people of all ages, races, and economic backgrounds.

An interesting aspect of Cuban culture is the love for classical music. I mentioned earlier that my natural father was a musician. He eventually became the director of the Orquesta Filarmónica de La Habana. His brother Jorge Bolet was a world class pianist, who was ranked as one of the top one hundred pianists in the twentieth century.

The Philharmonic Orchestra, together with the private Sociedad Pro-Arte Musical[3] promoted classical music and ballet in Cuba. Many prominent classical composers and performers came from this tradition. World renowned prima ballerina Alicia Alonso, composer Ernesto Lecuona and his sister Ernestina, Gonzalo Roig, and Jorge Ackerman are all additional examples of superb classical musicians from Cuba.

---

[3] Sociedad Pro-Arte Musical - founded in 1918, this non-profit organization promoted the career of Cuban musical talent and gave concerts in many venues. The Society staged works by world talented musicians, examples include Jasha Heifitz, Vladimir Horowitz, Sergei Rachmaninoff, Renata Tebaldi and Andrés Segovia among many others.

Image 4: *Claudio José Brindis de Sala*

Love of classical music was not a new trend. There were many prominent classical musicians at the turn of the century: José White and Claudio José Brindis de Sala[4] are two examples that come to mind. Claudio José Brindis de Sala was an internationally acclaimed violinist who attended the Paris Conservatory and won the First Prize. He played in the best European concert halls and received numerous awards and decorations including the French Legion d'Honneur and the Prussian Order of the Black Eagle.

---

[4] Claudio Brindis de Sala (1800-1850) was a Violinist and band leader. His son Claudio José Brindis de Sala attained many honors as a musician in Cuba and abroad. He performed in many European concert halls. He received the French Légion d'Honneur and was named a Baron by the German Kaiser.

Music and song were the lifeblood of Cuban culture. There was a uniqueness about Cuban culture that cut across social, economic and racial lines. Cubans were expected to have a gregarious and happy demeanor; the biggest social sin a person could commit was to be "un pesado"[5].

In my childhood I distinctly remember two events: I danced in the streets in el Carnaval de la Habana, and my family and I vacationed at la playa de Varadero.

El Carnaval de la Habana

Image 5: *Carnaval de La Habana*

---

[5] "un pesado" – literally "a person of heavy weight" – the real meaning of this term in Cuba was that you did not fit in, were anti-social, did not like to have fun, or did not fit in with the group.

Image 6: *Carnaval de La Habana*
**Many businesses and organizations sponsored "carrozas" (floats)
This one was sponsored by a Radio Station – Radio Progreso**

The experience of participating in the Carnaval de la Habana, held for three nights before Ash Wednesday annually, created such an impact on me that I can close my eyes and relive the feelings I had as a teenager decades ago.

The Carnaval was open to all and was held every year during the three days preceding Ash Wednesday. It consisted of public parades by organized neighborhood sponsored groups called comparsas, was intermixed with open cars, floats and trucks, and featured throngs of people singing, drinking, dancing, and having fun. A very Cuban thing to do was to "arrollar" in front of the comparsas letting yourself be immersed into the music and the fantastic percussion sound of hundreds of "tumbadoras" (Afro-Cuban percussion instruments ranging from very big conga drums to very small "timbales"); the music section also had all kinds of bells, trumpets, guiros, and other instruments peculiar to these groups. The sound was encompassing and seeped into your consciousness until you were one with the rest of the people on the street, becoming intoxicated with the sheer joy of it.

Different groups played short ditties that were set to conga music and were known by all. Here are some of the most popular.

"Tú que me decías que el Yayabo no salía más...." originated in the City of Sancti Spiritus and took its name from the Yayabo river that ran through the center of town.

"Al carnaval, de Oriente me voy, donde mejor, se puede gozar..." This one referred to the Carnaval de Santiago de Cuba, Cuba's second largest city and host to the second most famous carnaval on the island.

Las Jardineras

I liked to find a particular comparsa which always had fantastic costumes, music and a very traditional way to arrollar, and join the crowd following them. The comparsa Las Jardineras[6] was our favorite, they came from a very poor area of La Habana (El Barrio de Jesús María) and always put on a great show. They had a fantastic percussion section and their beat was like the pulse of a gigantic living being.

Image 7: *Comparsa Las Jardineras – Carnaval de la Habana*

---

[6] Las Jardineras – the ladies that take care of the flowers...

Some people liked to go to the carnaval in convertibles or open trucks, my brother and I liked to walk with the crowd and arrollar with the people.

You had found the Jardineras when you heard their signature song:

"Flores, flores, ahí vienen las jardineras vienen regando flores…"

In addition to the crowd and the costumes, many comparsas had farolas (a Cuban fixture of the comparsa consisting of a decorated pole topped by an antique light fixture that was twirled by a comparsa member), as well as floats with members dancing on the beds of trucks or trailers.

The really good comparsas could be spectacular, the Chinese horns would produce their unique sound and the comparsa and the people arrollando around it, would become a distinct living organism, all who were a part of it moving down the Malecón and the Paseo del Prado Boulevard like one huge musical dragon, inebriating all who became a part of it.

La Playa de Varadero

Image 8: *Playa de Varadero – Provincia de Matanzas, Cuba*

I have traveled throughout the world and have never seen a beach as perfectly beautiful. The sand is white powder; the water is the color of an amazingly clear turquoise. A person can wade through crystal clear shallow water for seemingly endless kilometers. The Cuban sky is so blue that its only description approaches the infinite. The water was always at a perfect temperature and allowed bathing year round.

The weather was fantastic during most of the year. My brother and I learned to swim here. My step father threw us off at the end of the pier in the Cawama Hotel when I was six years old. Fear of sharks did the rest.

Varadero was one example of the natural beauty prevalent throughout our island, the largest in the Caribbean. The subtropical climate and exposure to the ocean on all sides moderated the weather and made possible an outdoor lifestyle year round.

There were many beach homes, hotels, and amenities (restaurants, a very large marina, etc.) in Varadero. It was the prime destination for newlyweds on the island.

El Colegio de La Salle

Image 9: *Colegio de la Salle de Miramar – Primera Avenida entre Calle 32 y Calle 34 Miramar, La Habana, Cuba*

I went to elementary school at the Colegio de La Salle de Miramar. It was a Catholic school staffed by Los Hermanos de La Salle[7]. I received a fantastic education involving extensive instruction in mathematics, science, religion, foreign languages, the classics, and the arts. My favorite subjects were history and mathematics. Los Hermanos believed in a balanced approach to education, the importance of discipline, personal initiative, and the value of physical education. We participated in sports (baseball being very popular).

Image 10: My brother Armando, our sister Sylvita and I before a football game

---

[7] La Salle Brothers – known in the US as the Christian Brothers, this religious order was founded in 1684 by Saint John Baptist de la Salle, a priest living in Reims, France. Its original mission was to provide quality education to all children, particularly the poor.

My brother Armando and I played football for La Salle. We played both offense and defense in those days, and I loved to play middle linebacker. We also played baseball at school. I played second and right field. My brother was a much better athlete than I, but I was very competitive and liked sports. I also swam in the Profesionales swimming team.

Life at school was not all studies and sports. I like to tell my children and grandchildren a story about an actual incident that happened when I was in fifth grade involving my teacher, El Hermano Luis. He was over six feet tall and probably weighed well over 200 pounds. He could fonguear[8] a baseball over the school's back fence which was well over 80 meters from the home plate. He was idolized by the children.

On this particular morning we were walking to the nearest Catholic Church, Santa Rita, and passed a group of construction workers digging a ditch in the street. Some of them made the mistake of jeering at our teacher. They called out insulting phrases such as: "Ey, mariquita, quitate las sotana, maricon..."[9]

He stood there for a moment and then took off his sotana[10] and jumped in the ditch. He beat the literal hell out of the loudest construction worker, who defended himself well. When he saw the worker on the ground covering his face, he stopped and without saying a word, jumped back on the sidewalk, put his cassock back on and turned to us and said:

"Come on, don't just stand there, we'll be late for mass!"

From that moment on, Hermano Luis could do no wrong. He was an icon in the entire school, more popular than any singer or baseball star.

---

[8] Cuban term for a type of batting practice. This consisted of throwing a baseball up in the air from a standing position and batting it on the way down.

[9] Hey, little homo, take off your robe you queer...

[10] Sotana was the brothers' cassock; it was a long black robe with a peculiar white collar.

Lessons in Cuban History I Learned in School

Image 11: *General Antonio Maceo y Grajales*

Cuba waged three wars of independence against Spain. The first one started in 1868 when a wealthy landowner from Oriente Province set all his slaves free and started an armed insurrection against Spanish colonial rule. The principal figures in this war were Carlos Manuel de Céspedes, Ignacio Agramonte, Cirilo Villaverde, Antonio Maceo, Máximo Gómez and a young writer sentenced to prison, José Martí, who would later become the heart of the independence movement and die in battle at Dos Ríos, Oriente Province.

One of the country's most revered heroes was Antonio Maceo, who was nicknamed El Titán de Bronce.[11] He fought in all three

---

[11] General Antonio Maceo fought in all three wars of independence from Spain. Starting in 1868 and ending in the independence war of 1895 where the

of these wars and was admired by all Cubans. In our Cuban history textbooks and lessons he was a founding father alongside other freedom fighters and important historical figures such as José Martí, Carlos Manuel de Céspedes, and Máximo Gómez. Antonio Maceo was also viewed as a martyr, a very courageous man, and a member of an exemplary family who sacrificed their lives to bring independence to Cuba. I admired him greatly for his courage and determination (Foner).

The third and final war, named appropriately La Guerra de Independencia[12] started in 1895 and lasted until 1898, when the United States declared war on Spain after the Battleship USS Maine suffered an inexplicable catastrophe in the harbor of La Habana. My great grandfather on my mother's side fought in this war. He was the aide-de-camp to General Juan Rius Rivera and was killed in action crossing the Trocha from Mariel to Majana in Pinar del Rio Province.[13]

On February 15, 1898 a mysterious explosion sank the battleship USS Maine in La Habana harbor while it was conducting a visit to "show the US support for independence for Cuba." No explanation was provided by the Spanish authorities and the US declared war on Spain on April 21, 1898. The US intervened militarily in the Philippines, Cuba, Puerto Rico, and the island of Guam.

US intervened in 1898 during the Spanish American war. El titan de bronze means the bronze titan. Maceo was killed in combat on the 7th of December of 1897.

[12] Guerra de Independencia - War for Independence. Cuba was a protectorate of the US from 1898 to 1902 when it was finally granted its independence. The US and the Cuban constitution of 1902 were amended by US Senator Platt who introduced a clause giving the US the right to intervene in Cuban affairs if the interests of the US were affected. Although the Platt amendment was never formally invoked, it was widely resented in Cuba and provided the communist government of Fidel Castro with ammunition for his anti-American propaganda.

[13] Trocha de Mariel a Majana - a fortified line of Spanish forts and troops intended to cut access from Pinar del Rio to the rest of the island. There were two other similar Trochas on the eastern end of the Island.

After the almost complete obliteration of the Spanish Navy and landings by US forces in Cuba, the Philippines, and Puerto Rico, Spain capitulated to the US on December 10, 1898. The Treaty of Paris stipulated that Spain cede the Philipine Islands, Cuba, Puerto Rico, and Guam to the United States.

The United States appointed a governor, Leonard C. Wood, who set out to reconstruct Cuba's infrastructure, build schools, and implement an extensive effort to eradicate yellow fever which continued to claim thousands of lives. He also started a process to draft a new constitution and began to hold local elections at the municipal level. Leonard C. Wood is a figure that is unjustly ignored in current historical accounts. His contributions to reconstruct Cuban infrastructure, develop educational institutions, and advances in Public Health created a feeling of hope and gratitude towards the United States.

In 1902 the Stars and Stripes were lowered over the fortresses of El Morro and La Cabana and the United States military left Cuba which became a sovereign nation.

My family was involved in that transition. Members of the Vidal and Bacallao family from Cardenas were attorneys and served with the Cuban staff involved in the drafting of the 1902 Constitution. I remember my two great aunts, María and Blanca Vidal, telling us stories about the US fleet bombing Cardenas harbor in 1898 and how tough life became during that time. Their love for Cuba was visible and very strong. They had a deep influence in my life.

Summers in the US

My uncle on my mother's side, Pedro Suarez, was very wealthy. When he was young and very poor, his sisters gave him a sum of money out of their inheritance, so he could go to college. He became a very successful civil engineer and paid back many times over the help they had given him to get his start.

When I was thirteen my parents decided to send me to a military school in Indiana for the summer. My uncle paid for it. This was my initiation to American life, language, and culture in the mid nineteen fifties. I loved every second of it.

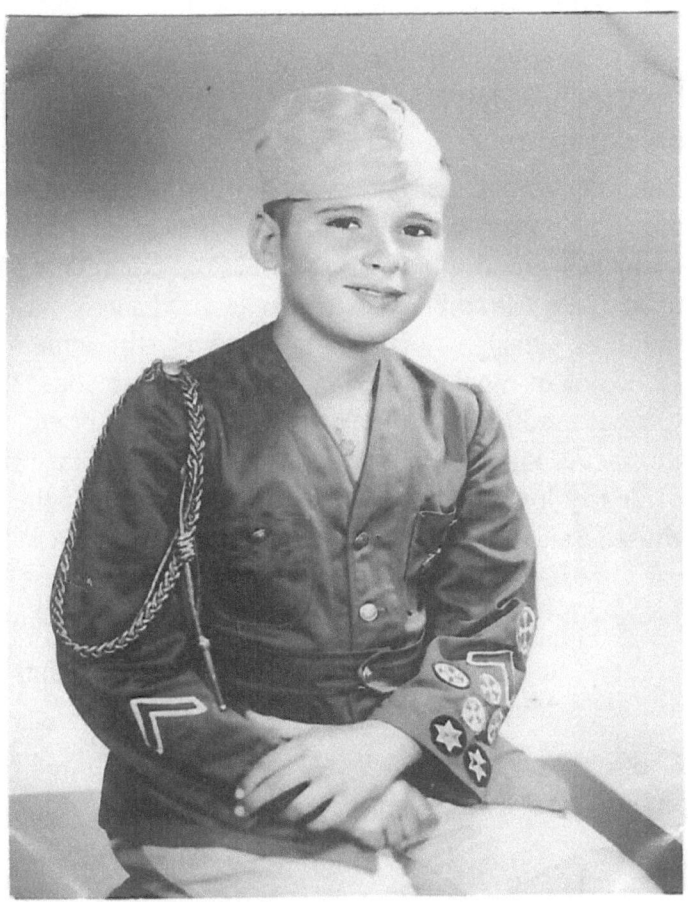

Image 12: *Summer School – Culver Military Academy*

At Culver I learned many useful skills. I speak English as a native today with a Midwestern accent because of it. Culver was a military academy staffed at that time primarily by retired military personnel, many of them with combat experience in WWII and the Korean War.

We sang cadence songs while marching in formation, I remember two:

"We were fighting in Korea, getting full of gonorrhea, sound off – one two, sound off – three four, cadence count – a one and a two and a three and a four and a one two – three four!"

Here is the other:

"The WAVES and the WACS are winning the war, so what the hell are we fighting for - sound off...."

In the Summer school, I attended the Woodcraft and then the naval summer program and my brother went to the Black Horse Troop camp. I learned to sail on the fleet of sailboats the Academy had on Lake Maxinkuckee. I also learned many navy traditions including naval history, signal flags (I still remember the shape and color of most naval signal flags), Morse code, the phonetic alphabet used by the military in WWII (alpha, bravo, charlie, delta, etc.) naval knots and many other practical military skills. A subject I dearly loved was world history, in particular the history of the United States Military in the two World Wars.

But most importantly I learned the values of the greatest generation, so sorely missing in today's educational system in America:

> Honesty, integrity, truthfulness, responsibility, initiative, love of country, and love of God.

I loved both my native country of Cuba **and** the United States. I loved both of them with the same level of intensity.

LA REVOLUCIÓN

January 1, 1959 was the watershed. Before that day life was "normal", there were political parties fighting for power, there was injustice and abuse, but in Cuba there was an old saying "la isla de Cuba está hecha de corcho, esto no lo hunde nadie."[14] All that was about to change. On January 1, 1959, I saw the mobs rampage through our neighborhood looking for houses of prominent Batista government members and looting them. They left everyone in our street alone with the exception of a house on the corner, the home of a Batista politician. They took everything of value, but left much of their extensive book collection lying on the street.

This behavior, unfortunately, was to be typical of the brutal and ignorant nature of the majority of the officers involved in the Communist regime led by Fidel Castro. I will describe later on examples of this as it relates to the treatment of captured Brigade members and of the rural population caught in the guerrilla movement in the Escambray mountains and elsewhere. Loyalty alone, absent of talent, experience, or education, was prized and rewarded by the regime. This would contribute to the economic and social collapse of the island.

Fidel Castro and the 26th of July Movement

Fidel's Youth

Fidel Castro was a middle class young man from Cuba's Oriente Province. He attended the Jesuit prep school, Colegio de Belen in La Habana. Belen was one of the finest schools in the country.

---

[14] Luis Machado (a Cuban economist) wrote an essay titled "La Isla de Corcho, Ensayo de la Economía Cubana" in 1936. He wanted to understand why the standard of living was adequate for the poorest Cubans in the middle of a severe economic depression

My father-in-law's family, the Celorios, went to Belen at the same time Fidel was a high school student there. My father-in-law's brother, Felo Celorio, was in Fidel's class. His main memory of Fidel is that he practiced public speaking using translations of Benito Mussolini's speeches in an open area.

Fidel and Felo were members of the track team. Felo beat Fidel in a race once. Fidel was so enraged that he chased him around the track field with a small revolver yelling that he was going to kill him.

Image 13: *Belen Track Team - Fidel Castro (2nd row from bottom on the right) and Felo Celorio (bottom row)*

When Fidel graduated from Belen, he was admitted to the Universidad de La Habana - Facultad de Derecho[15], the best in the nation at that time.

Fidel Castro's main activity at the university was revolutionary politics.

In 1947 he joined an abortive attempt by leftist Cuban students and Dominican exiles to invade the Dominican Republic and overthrow Gen. Rafael Trujillo, who was, at that time, the current dictator. This abortive invasion failed to materialize.

In 1948, while he was a law student at the University of La Habana, Fidel Castro was involved in a plot to assassinate the leader of the FEU[16] Manolo Castro. He was widely recognized, but never convicted of being the trigger man in the killing of this student leader. This permissiveness and belief in the violent removal of opposition was to become yet another typical symptom of the injustices present within the Castro regime.

In April 1948 Fidel took part in a communist supported coup attempt to overthrow the Columbian government that broke out in Bogotá, Colombia. He was there with a group of young radical students from various Latin American countries with Marxist leanings. This incident failed after much bloodshed and would be widely published by newspapers in Latin America. The failed revolution started with the assassination of a prominent Colombia presidential candidate, Eliecer Gaitan; the assassination was followed by riots, looting, and a bloody melee culminating in the burning of a large portion of downtown Bogota. The event is known in Colombian history as El Bogotazo (Brown & Kline).

---

[15] Universidad de la Habana - Facultad de Derecho – University of Habana - School of Law

[16] FEU – Federacion Estudiantil Universitaria – Powerful student government organization in the University of La Habana, it played many leadership roles in political protests in Cuba starting in the 1930's with the deposition of President Machado.

What was a middle class Cuban university law student doing in Colombia participating in this type of revolt? A question the bureaucrats at the State Department never answered satisfactorily and very unwisely chose to overlook while investigating Castro.

The US media has for many years peddled the lie that Fidel was not a communist when he assumed power on January 1, 1959. This was blatantly false. His brother Raúl was a member of the communist party when he was a university student. Castro's personal background and prior involvement in political unrest in the Caribbean and the Americas demonstrated his psychopathic and violent tendencies, which he masked behind the façade of the communist political ideology.

His best friend and right-hand man, Che Guevara was a supporter of the first communist government in the Americas, headed by Jacobo Arbenz in Guatemala. Arbenz was married to an avowed communist, María Vilanova, who introduced him to Marx and Engel and converted him to communism. He appointed many communists to positions of power in his administration and introduced in Guatemala, much of the type of legislation that Che copied when he came to power in Cuba: agrarian reform, student indoctrination, and confiscation of local and foreign investment were examples of communist practices Che implemented in Cuba.

Ernesto (Che) Guevara was born in Argentina to very wealthy parents. His father was a prominent doctor in Buenos Aires. The media treated Che Guevara with the same ignorance it treated Castro. Guevara was a bloodthirsty killer who personally participated in the executions of "criminals" and who dictated many death sentences involving young anti-communist counter-revolutionaries who were arrested by the secret police.

The US media and academic institutions, even today, romanticize Guevara as a young political radical fighting injustice on behalf of the poor, and hide his violent tendencies and blood-thirsty nature. This is evident in popular literature included in academic institutions and in films propagating communist political theory such as *The Motorcycle Diaries*.

In Guatemala Guevara was a young foreign doctor who threw himself into politics to defend Arbenz's policies. These policies had the effect of creating opposition among US corporations, the US State Department, and many other foreign countries investing in Guatemala.

The CIA provided aid to conservative elements of the Guatemalan military, and Arbenz was deposed in a coup led by Colonel Carlos Castillo Armas. This coup was supported by the CIA and one of its principal planners was Jacob Esterline, who was deputy chief of the CIA Task Force code named PBSUCCESS that planned the operation. As we will see later in this book, Esterline was also involved in planning the Bay of Pigs operation. Arbenz and many of his advisors, including Che Guevara, fled Guatemala and applied for political exile in Mexico ("Jacobo Arbenz").

Insights Into the Truth about the Cuban Revolution

Before continuing reading, I will ask you to try to not be influenced by any media accounts you may have read or heard about the Revolution in Cuba. Also be wary of sites like "Wikipedia" who allow the Cuban government to control the historical messages and posts. Please visit the Media Research Center website listed in the Bibliography Appendix to understand the ongoing campaign to lie to the world about the facts surrounding the Communist Regime in Cuba.

The Cuban Revolution, in order to topple the unconstitutional Batista dictatorship,[17] had to obtain broad support in Cuban society.

---

[17] Fulgencio Batista Saldivar was an ex Cuban military NCO (sergeant) who assisted the rebels in the 1933 coup that deposed Cuban President Machado. In 1940 he was elected president of Cuba, served his term and left the country. He

The primary active force of the opposition consisted of the students in the Universidad de la Habana. The university student's organization called FEU[18] bore the brunt of Batista's police and military repressive organizations during the period 1952 to 1958. Their most spectacular action was the Asalto a Palacio (assault on the presidential palace) on 13 March 1957, a commando operation that attacked the Presidential Palace with the objective of assassinating President Batista combined with the commandeering of a very popular news radio station in La Habana, Radio Reloj, to announce the success of the attack. Batista narrowly escaped the attackers. The security forces of Batista then proceeded to kill all captured attackers and many opposition members who had ties to the attackers. The FEU's opposition preceded the 26th of July movement led by Fidel and his brother Raúl. The FEU at that time, had no ideological ties with the 26th of July movement or the communist party.

The overwhelming majority of FEU students were **not** members of the communist party. Many of the leaders of political parties and organizations that opposed Batista (Partido Autentico, Partido Ortodoxo, CTC - Confederación de Trabajadores Cubanos)[19] were not ideological communists.

There was a small communist party in Cuba led by a former union leader turned communist, Blas Roca. This person was not popular and did not actively participate in the anti-Batista movement.

The 26th of July movement was one of many guerrilla and resistance groups fighting Batista in the Cuban mountains. They falsely claimed later to have single-handedly carried out the revolution that toppled Batista. This myth was initiated during the

---

lived in the US until he returned to Cuba in 1950. With the support of some key high ranking officers in the Cuban military, he assumed power by staging a coup d'etat on March 10, 1952

[18] FEU – Federacion Estudiantil Universitaria – University Students Federation

[19] CTC – Confederation of Cuban Workers – Largest Cuban labor union, their largest membership group were sugar cane workers. Cuba had many active and powerful labor unions. There are no labor unions in Cuba today.

waning years of the Batista government by the propaganda arm of the July 26th movement and faithfully fed to the world by the US media. Primary actors in this shameful deception were Jules DuBois, of the Chicago Tribune and President of the Inter American Press Society and Herbert Mathews, a reporter for the New York Times. For years these individuals crafted an image of Fidel as a sort of Robin Hood like figure who would bring equality to the suffering Cuban guajiros[20].

This image is repulsive on many levels, Cuba was a modern and prosperous country, the guajiros in Cuba for the most part did not care for politics and the majority were gainfully employed, many cultivated their own plots of land for their consumption and sold the surplus, many others worked for large agribusinesses such as the Centrales Azucareros[21] or for widely diversified and Cuban owned agricultural businesses (fincas with large plantings of rice, citrus, produce, and tropical fruits). Other large agribusinesses with significant operations who employed a large number of people, were cattle ranches, poultry farms, and tobacco planting and cigar manufacturing for which Cuba was world famous. A large majority of these guajiros owned their own plot of land. The output of these businesses all satisfied Cuban internal demand and by the early fifties produced surpluses that were exported to other markets throughout the Americas. I do not want to imply that there was no poverty in Cuba (there was) or that all guajiros lived happy blissful lives (they had to work very hard to subsist) but the majority had enough to eat and were not burdens to the state.

Any one that continues to approve of Castro's actions after assuming power is either ignorant of the facts or a sympathizer of the Soviet and Chinese communist economic models. The leftist claims that Fidel wanted democracy and a return to constitutional

---

[20] Guajiros - nickname for Cuban agricultural workers or Cubans that lived in rural areas.

[21] Centrales Azucareros – Large Sugar Mills that were surrounded by sugar cane plantations. Most of these mills were owned by Cuban families or corporations.

government in Cuba are patently false. I hope that the facts outlined in this book will help many to realize that they have been influenced by a vast worldwide movement that uses deceit and groupthink to influence public opinion.

Cuba's Descent Into Tyranny

Armas Para Que?[22]

Image 14: *Castro hugs Khrushchev*

---

[22] Armas Para Que? For what purpose do you need weapons?

On January 8 1959, fresh from his triumphant victory tour following President Batista's flight into exile, Fidel Castro and his "barbudos"[23] drove into the capital of La Habana driving captured Cuban Army Jeeps, Trucks and Tanks.

That night Fidel gave the first of many night-long tirades. The intent was to bypass government institutions and to make the people directly answerable to him. The theme of the first speech was that all weapons legally held by Cuban citizens must be turned into the revolutionary army, they were not needed any more.

Fidel, his brother Raúl and their communist advisor Che Guevara, immediately started to dismantle the constitutional government of Cuba and its many institutions.

The highest priority was given to the elimination of the professional security forces in Cuba, the constitutionally created armed forces: army, air force and navy, the municipal police departments, and the rural Guardia Civil. All career officers in these organizations lost their jobs, were persecuted, many accused, some of real, but many of false crimes and many executed in the infamous "Roman Circus" like trials where the outcome was predetermined: "al paredon," which translates to: "take them to the execution wall and execute them".[24]

All laws and institutions protecting individual rights were ignored. The Castro government proclaimed that they had blanket authority to detain, confiscate property and deny individuals any avenue to appeal dictates by government officials.

---

[23] Barbudos – the bearded ones – most of the Guerrillas who fought in the Cuban mountains did not shave and sported full beards.

[24] I had two uncles who were officers in the armed forces. Antonio Bolet, who served in the Ejército Constitucional de Cuba (retired), and Domingo Bolet, an officer in the Policía Nacional (Cuban Police). They both suffered this type of persecution and eventually were forced to go into exile.

The Destruction of the Cuban Economy

In researching this segment of Cuban history I found a large number of links to US media sites trying to peddle a Marxist interpretation of pre-Castro economic conditions. If you link to these sites and read their content, what you will see is the communist party line, that Cuba was full of US Mafia owned casinos and that the majority of Cuban women were prostitutes. These articles written by Castro sympathizers also state that Castro revived the Cuban economy. Nothing could be further from the truth than the propaganda that is accepted as gospel in many universities and so called think tanks.

Here is a quote from the Journal For Economic History:

We examine Cuban GDP over time and across space. We find that Cuba was once a prosperous middle-income economy. On the eve of the revolution, incomes were 50 to 60 percent of European levels. They were among the highest in Latin America at about 30 percent of the United States. In relative terms, Cuba was richer earlier on. Income per capita during the 1920s was in striking distance of Western Europe and the Southern United States. After the revolution, Cuba slipped down to the bottom of the world income distribution rankings. Current levels of income per capita appear well below their pre-revolutionary peaks.[25]

Why Socialism Never Works

Top Down Planning

When we were living in DC, my wife and I became friends of Jorge Beruff who used to be the director of the Cuban Bank for

---

[25] The Journal of Economic History Vol. 72, No. 1 (MARCH 2012), pp. 104-133 Published By: Cambridge University Press

Economic Development (a unit of the Banco Nacional de Cuba[26]). When Castro took power he appointed Ernesto (Che) Guevara as President of the Banco Nacional de Cuba. Guevara was also in charge of the Agrarian Reform which was implemented through the Ministerio del Interior (Interior Ministry). He loved to tell a story that highlights the failures of Socialism when implemented by oligarchs.

Here is Jorge Beruff's story as told to my wife Margarita and I:

"The government had ordered the purchase of hundreds of thousands of pounds of fertilizer to distribute to state run farms. The ship arrived in the Port of La Habana and the captain requested instruction as to unloading the cargo. No one dared to respond and the query went all the way to the top. Che, who was the President of National Bank of Cuba and who had never had a real job in his life, ordered the fertilizer (which was stored in paper bags) to be unloaded immediately. The captain quickly complied so he could turn the ship around and sail home.

The next day there were two or three thunderstorms (this was very normal as it was the rainy season). This weather pattern continued for the next few days. When the railroad cars finally came to load the fertilizer it was ruined and had to be thrown away. This cost the government millions of dollars. Why did this happen? Anyone with any common sense could have picked up the phone and told Che the fertilizer was going to be ruined, but no one had the guts to do it."

These problems were common in the overwhelming majority of the private businesses that were "nationalized". The people that were put in charge were selected for their "revolutionary" merits; none of them knew anything about the business or industry they were supposed to lead. The second problem was their educational level, most of them had little or no formal education.

---

[26] Banco Nacional de Cuba – Cuba's National Bank, a central bank that had the power to regulate economic and fiscal policy in Cuba

But the media ignores the big elephant in the room, the answer to the question:

Why does Socialism never work?

People that are asked to manage these state assets have no vested interest in doing their jobs well. Humans always treasure and protect what belongs to them or to their family. Fear is a great motivator to destroy, never to build or create.....

Universal Health Care

One of the recurring lies propagated by the liberal media is the advancement made by the Cuban revolution in Health Care. The following quote is from a US State Dept Evaluation made during the Obama administration:

The [Cuban] health care system is often touted by many analysts as one of the Castro government's greatest achievements. What this analysis ignores is that the revolutionary government inherited an already-advanced health sector when it took power in 1959.

Cuba's infant mortality rate of 32 per 1,000 live births in 1957 was the lowest in Latin America and the 13th lowest in the world, according to UN data. Cuba ranked ahead of France, Belgium, West Germany, Israel, Japan, Austria, Italy, and Spain, all of which would eventually pass Cuba in this indicator during the following decades.

Cuba's comparative world ranking according to data in Table 1 has fallen from 13th to LAST *out of the 25 countries examined. Also missing from the conventional analysis of Cuba's infant mortality rates is its staggering abortion rate of 77.7 abortions per 1,000 women aged 15-44 in 1996 -- which, because of selective termination of "high-risk" pregnancies, yields lower numbers for infant mortality. Cuba's abortion rate was the 3rd highest out of the 60 countries studied.*

In terms of physicians and dentists per capita, Cuba in 1957 ranked third in Latin America, behind only Uruguay and

Argentina -- both of which were more advanced than the United States in this measure. Cuba's 128 physicians and dentists per 100,000 people in 1957 was the same as the Netherlands, and ahead of the United Kingdom (122 per 100,000 people) and Finland (96).[27]

In recent years the Universidad de la Habana has adopted programs where they graduate students in two years using a curriculum limited to treatment of tropical diseases and issue a Medical Doctorate diploma upon completion. The objective is to place these "Doctors" in foreign countries and receive revenue in hard currencies (Dollars or Euros) for their services. These Doctors are also required to indoctrinate their patients on the benefits of socialism.

Agriculture

It is hard to describe the absolute economic debacle brought about by the confiscation of all privately owned farms (of any size) and the forced relocation of agricultural workers to state owned and operated farms. The results in terms of reduction of crop yields and overall productivity were disastrous. One exception was the sugar industry during the period 1965 to 1990. During that period the government mobilized the entire country to work in the sugar industry in an effort to increase the sugar cane harvest. Fidel's goal was to obtain a harvest of 10 million tons even though this goal was theoretically impossible to achieve given existing sugar mill capacity. That effort failed even though civilians from all walks of life were continuously trucked to sugar communes to help harvest the crop.

If you look at the numbers in the following table detailing Cuban sugar production and exports, in the period from 1959 to 1964 you will see declines in production and yield even though this was

---

[27] Zenith and Eclipse: A Comparative Look at Socio-Economic Conditions in Pre-Castro and Present Day Cuba - Released by the Bureau of Inter-American Affairs, February 9, 1998. Revised June 2002

the national focused area for government planners.[28] By the early 1990's production had slipped well below pre-revolution 1950's levels.

Table 1. Cuba: Sugar Production and Exports (thousands of metric tons)

Year	Production	Exports	% Exp.
1955	4,528.00	4,644.00	102.56%
1956	4,740.00	5,394.00	113.80%
1957	5,672.00	5,307.00	93.56%
1958	5,784.00	5,632.00	97.37%
1959	5,964.00	4,952.00	83.03%
1960	5,862.00	5,635.00	96.13%
1961	6,767.00	6,414.00	94.78%
1962	4,815.00	5,131.00	106.56%
1963	3,821.00	3,521.00	92.15%
1964	4,590.00	4,176.00	90.98%
1965	6,082.00	5,316.00	87.41%
1966	4,867.00	4,435.00	91.12%
1967	6,236.00	5,683.00	91.13%
1968	5,315.20	4,613.00	86.79%
1969	5,534.18	4,798.82	86.71%
1970	7,558.56	6,906.29	91.37%
1971	5,950.03	5,510.86	92.62%
1972	5,687.80	4,139.56	72.78%
1973	5,382.55	4,797.38	89.13%
1974	5,925.85	5,491.25	92.67%
1975	6,427.38	5,743.71	89.36%
1976	6,150.80	5,763.65	93.71%
1977	6,953.28	6,238.16	89.72%
1978	7,661.55	7,231.22	94.38%
1979	7,799.97	7,269.43	93.20%
1980	6,805.24	6,191.07	90.98%
1981	7,925.63	7,071.45	89.22%
1982	8,039.48	7,734.28	96.20%
1983	7,460.23	6,792.09	91.04%
1984	7,783.41	7,016.51	90.15%
1985	7,889.24	7,209.01	91.38%
1986	7,467.42	6,702.59	89.76%
1987	7,231.77	6,482.14	89.63%
1988	8,119.05	6,978.22	85.95%
1989	7,579.01	7,123.31	93.99%
1990	8,444.70	7,171.76	84.93%
1991	7,233.39	6,767.46	93.56%
1992	7,218.80	6,084.88	84.29%
1993	4,245.72	3,661.96	86.25%
1994	3,994.00	3,264.00	81.72%
1995	3,300.00	2,568.00	77.82%
Annual Average	6,263.71	5,696.64	90.95%

Table 1. Sugar Production and Exports – Pre Revolution (1955-1958) and Post Revolution (1959 to1995)

---

[28] Association for the Study of the Cuban Economy – November 30, 1995

Prior to the revolution Cuba was an exporter of surplus food products including beef, rice, produce, fruits and seafood. Today there are food lines and scarcity in an island where a common joke was: *Throw any seed to the ground and it will grow.*

Foreign Relations

Image 15: *The visit that rattled the Eisenhower State Dept*

Anastas Mikoyan, Foreign Minister of the Soviet Union visited Cuba in February, 1960 (Fidel assumed power in January 1959). On the 16 th of February, Cuba and the USSR signed an agreement where the Soviets would purchase 5 million tons of Cuban sugar over a five year period and lend Cuba 100 million dollars at 2.5 percent interest rate. This was perfectly legal and should raise no eyebrows except that Cuba had never in its history, done business with the Soviet Union. In addition they discussed other topics including Soviet arm sales to Cuba, specifically touching on the sale of MIG aircraft for the Cuban FAR.[29]

During this initial period of the Revolution, the Cuban government started to 'nationalize' (steal) the assets of many internation-

---

[29] FAR - Fuerza Aérea Revolucionaria - Revolutionary Air Force

al corporations operating in Cuba. This was a gradual program that eventually confiscated all private property in Cuba and placed ownership of farms, residences and businesses in the hands of the state. United States policy toward Cuba was immediately reversed since many of these businesses were owned by American corporations.

Exodus

More than one million Cubans (Cuba had a population of over six million people in 1959) went into exile not only to the US, but also to many other Latin American and European countries in the first five years following Fidel's rise to power. **The reasons were not economic**.

Religious and Private schools were closed. Priests and religious orders were expelled from Cuba. Thousands of Cuban mothers entrusted their children to strangers in the United States[30] so their children would have the chance to escape the indoctrination of the new Cuban revolutionary educational system.

Increasingly large numbers of people lost their businesses and their homes as the communist system gradually expropriated small privately owned businesses and private homes by passing a number of so-called reform laws.

The Castro dictatorship also abolished the Cuban Constitution and replaced all Cuban democratic institutions with a Soviet and Chinese based communist system.

This exodus has continued until our present date and has been classified by US Government and Private Research institutions into distinct waves over a period covering the last sixty years. Many Cubans have risked and lost their lives in efforts to flee the

---

[30] Operation Peter Pan was organized by Father Bryan O Walsh, Director of Catholic Welfare Services in the US and James Baker, headmaster of an American school in Cuba – over 14,000 children were sent by their parents to Miami and relocated to private homes all over the US.

island using all kinds of conveyances, including rafts, boats of all kinds and sizes, inner tubes and other bizarre methods.

It must be noted that the majority of exiles after 1962 were not affluent members of the middle class, they were fully integrated and indoctrinated members of the Cuban proletariat or were expelled during the Mariel Boatlift because of health, age, criminal status or disability of some kind that prevented them from working at their assigned tasks.

Reign of Terror

Another sinister trend during these early years of the Revolution involved the expanded reach of the Castro Political Security Forces. A large number of civilians[31] who opposed the government were arrested and many executed by the Revolutionary repressive organizations like the DIER[32] or the Ejército Revolucionario – Sección G-2[33] The real numbers will never be known due to secrecy and lack of record keeping in these organizations. The G2 was formed under the leadership of Ramiro Valdez - a bloodthirsty murderer, responsible for the arrest and execution of thousands of Cubans throughout the island.[34]

---

[31] We will never know the actual numbers since these forces were staffed by people who were not professionals, and who were motivated in many instances by revenge, greed or lust

[32] DIER Directorio de Investigaciones del Ejército Revolucionario – Directory of Investigations of the Rebel Army Created in the early 1960's initially to identify ex Batista government members that were members of the counter revolution, was later absorbed into the much larger Departamento de Seguridad del Estado.

[33] G2 – Departamento para la Seguridad del Estado del Ejército Rebelde – (Department of State Security of the Rebel Army) Created in 1959 to spy on Cuban's opposing the Castro government or that could be a threat to his leadership.

[34] Ramiro Valdez - Has held numerous posts in Castro's dictatorship - a hatchet man for the government and responsible for the Cuban espionage activities and in command of the "security" forces sent to Venezuela to cement the com-

Image 16: *One of many 'fusilamientos' conducted by the revolution in the period 1959-1961*

The revolution also created secret "Comites de Barrio"[35] One could exist in every block in large cities and villages although initially you did not know where the one in your area was. Their function was to spy on their neighbors and report any anti-government comments or activity. Children were taught in school that it was OK to turn your parents in. Any report would speedily bring a night-time visit by the G2 or later the DIER or the dreaded Departamento de Seguridad del Estado. People who were accused would disappear and based on the results of a secret investigation, would either be eliminated or sent to a "revolutionary re-

---

munist governments of Chavez and Maduro Reference:https:// cubaconfidential.wordpress.com/tag/g2/

[35] Comite de Barrio – Neighborhood Committee – Cubans are very gregarious and over time everyone knew who were the "chivatos" (tattle tales) in their area.

education center" to spend years in agricultural work as slave labor[36]

Margarita and I had a very close friend in Atlanta that was kept prisoner in Cuba for many years in one of these camps. He is now deceased, a victim of inhaling toxic pesticide fumes in these camps from which he never fully recovered.

My Brother and I Leave Cuba for the First Time

Image 17: *Fontainebleau Hotel 1960*

My parents, like many other Cuban parents, were aware of the increasing level of lawlessness and violence on the island. They put my brother and I on a Cubana[37] flight to Miami in July 1959. I arrived in the US at the age of 18 with five dollars in my pocket (you were not allowed to take money out of Cuba after the revolu-

---

[36] The most notorious of these were operated by the government's UMAP (Unidades Militares Para la Ayuda a la Producción) Military Units to Aid Production – most homosexuals, prostitutes and vagrants were arrested and sent there in addition to the political dissidents.

[37] Cubana de Aviación – Cuba's national airline

tion). We lived in my uncle's apartment in Miami Beach, and slept on a couch in my uncle's apartment. I started going to school during the day and working at the Fontainebleau Hotel parking cars at night. My family had been guests at this hotel the year before, now I was working there for tips!! Life has ways of showing you that accumulating wealth should not be your primary goal!!

This was the first of many menial jobs I had to take to finance my life. Life took a decisive turn for the worst for us and I started to learn many of the lessons associated with the "start again at the bottom of the pile with nothing, and find a way to survive" lifestyle.

My brother and I attended, and I graduated from, Miami Beach Senior High School in the 1960 class. Even though I worked at night I managed to get good grades. Our transcripts from High School in Cuba were not sufficient to receive a High School Diploma in the US since we had to meet some additional requirements such as US History, English Literature courses, etc. I did not have to study too hard during my senior high school year in Miami Beach since my Cuban Bachillerato education subjects were much more advanced and provided me with all the content I needed to pass the exams for the tough subjects (math, physics, chemistry, etc.).

LIFE IN MIAMI 1959-1960

Image 18: *University of Miami College of Engineering Building - circa 1960*

My parents finally were able to leave Cuba in 1960. My step father could not practice as an engineer in the US but got a job as a draftsman for Mackey Corporation, a construction company that was building expressways in the Dade County area. I was admitted to the University of Miami, School of Civil Engineering. I was fortunate to be the recipient of a new scholarship aid program provided to Cuban political refugees and could afford to go to school without having to wait until I had enough money to pay my tuition. I started school during the fall term of 1960. I also joined the Air Force ROTC program. That fall I passed the medical exam that would allow me to receive flight training. I was very happy at UM and my life seemed to have returned to its previous stable happy state. But the storm clouds were becoming very numerous on my horizon.....

The CIA and the Miami Cuban Exile Community in 1959-1960

The second term of Eisenhower's presidency was marred by his poor health and evident hands-off attitude towards governing the country. Foreign affairs in small nations were allowed to be conducted by government bureaucrats, many with little knowledge of the realities in the countries where they were serving. The situation in Cuba during the last years of the Batista dictatorship and the disaster that followed his overthrow is a perfect example.

Image 19: *Fulgencio Batista and Earl Smith US ambassador to Cuba 1957-1959*

The Batista regime's relationships with Washington went from good to strained to dismal. After winning a staged election for a "second term" in 1956, Batista saw an increase in domestic opposition that resorted to all methods to try to oust him. In addition to the aforementioned attack on the Presidential Palace by the University Students Federation, and the 1956 attack on the Moncada barracks, there were an increasing number of terrorist attacks on movie theaters and other public places where explosive devices were detonated. They were followed by large-scale repressive raids by the police where suspects (many of them students) would disappear and later would turn up dead in desolate places. The

Cuban underground carried out some very visible operations, the one receiving a large amount of publicity was the kidnapping of World Champion Formula 1 car racer Juan Fangio who was participating in a Gran Prix event held in La Habana in 1958.

In June 1957, U.S. President Dwight Eisenhower appointed Earl E. T. Smith ambassador to Cuba, replacing Arthur Gardner.

Smith was a businessman **who had never held a diplomatic position and who did not speak Spanish**. On arrival, Smith was urged by his staff to leave La Habana in order to get a better feel of the country, which was in a state of turmoil. On a visit to Santiago de Cuba, Smith witnessed first-hand the public funeral and burial of Frank País, one of the leaders of the Movimiento 26 de Julio. There was a large crowd at the burial, and that convinced Smith that something had to be done about the dictatorship of Fulgencio Batista.

This is so ludicrous that I want to present you with an analogy

> Suppose you were surprised to receive a call from the Office of the President of the United States to inform you that he has appointed you to be ambassador of the US to Monrovia (fictional Caribbean island nation). After you tell the caller that this is a mistake since you have never been there, and are not a diplomat you ask him to please brief you on the government, economy and political situation there. You frantically start reading the papers for everything related to this place and find out that you will be the representative of Monrovia's most powerful ally (the US), their primary supplier of military equipment and main commercial partner. On top of that you find out that thousands of your fellow Americans live there and that thousands of American businesses have operated there for years. That the United States was instrumental in helping Monrovia obtain its independence. And much more worrisome, Monrovia is in the middle of an internal revolution involving several competing factions. The State Department then, as part of their briefing, asks you to talk to a leftist reporter that recently interviewed one of the rebel leaders there.

Would you be able to recommend a proper course of action based on these assumptions? Would you take the job knowing the chances you would succeed were near zero?

Remember, you do not speak the language, have never been there before and you are not a diplomat..... **This really happened**, except that it was not a fictional country, it was Cuba, a staunch US allied island nation, 90 miles from the US, inhabited by truly exceptional people.

Even Smith, who was not attuned to the history or nuances of the Cuban situation, was critical of what he perceived as Washington's ambivalent attitude towards the then large number of opposition groups and the State Department's support for the 26th of July movement led by Fidel Castro. He believed that his superiors at State and the CIA were underestimating the strength of the Communist Party influence on Castro and several of his key supporters. He became increasingly aware of facts that confirmed his suspicions that there were many bureaucrats in the State Department that were openly supportive of Fidel and his socialist leanings.[38]

The tragic point is this: There were many other groups and leaders fighting Batista, the United States government could have supported any one of these groups and spared Cuba and the world from the curse of communism in Latin America that spread like a cancer to other parts of the world

Batista packed 6 million dollars from the Cuban Treasury into a military aircraft and left the country on December 31, 1958. He received temporary asylum from his fellow dictator Rafael Leonidas Trujillo in the Dominican Republic. He had opened a bank account there where he had deposited 30 million dollars. He betrayed his supporters both political and military. He did this in

---

[38] Testimony of Earl E T Smith before the Senate's Judiciary Subcommittee Investigating the Administration of the Internal Security Act -Eighty Sixth Congress - Second Session - Part 9 - US Government Printing Office

secret, and exited Cuban public life abandoning his supporters and the island nation to its fate. He has not been missed.

US Policy Actions Related to Cuba 1959-60

Miami, Miami Beach and unincorporated Dade County had a population of roughly 890,000 people on January 1 1959[39]. The Miami airport saw an increasingly large number of passengers flying to and from Rancho Boyeros Airport in La Habana. Returning to Cuba were a large number of exiled Cuban families that fled to the US during the Batista dictatorship. Flying to the US were increasingly larger numbers of Cubans fleeing from the Castro dictatorship. The inbound number grew from a relatively low trickle during the first few months to a flood of people starting in the second half of 1959 and during all of 1960.

Image 20: *Multiple planeloads of refugees arrived in Miami every day during the 1960's*

---

[39] US Census 1960 adjusted www.census.gov

During the second half of 1959, the US Government began to come to the conclusion that they had a real problem on their hands with the increasing radicalization and Marxist leaning of the Cuban Government's internal and foreign policy.

The Dulles Brothers

Image 21: *John Foster Dulles and Allen Dulles – Secretary of State and CIA Director during the Eisenhower Administration*

During his first term, President Eisenhower had appointed John Foster Dulles and his brother Allen as Secretary of State and Director of the CIA. Both of these men were strong anti-communists and had been involved in making many critical decisions and implementing projects related to Western European and Japanese reconstruction, the creation of Nato and conduct of US diplomacy during the early stages of the cold war. They assumed the direction of the US response to Castro. There were some serious flaws in this last appointment.

Although few can argue that they were lacking in education or foreign service experience, both Allen and John Foster Dulles were experts in dealing with the reconstruction of Europe after World War II and the US response to the creation of the Soviet Empire and its expansion into other so-called non-aligned nations. Riding the wave of anti-colonial feelings sweeping the Globe in the post war period, the Soviet Union soon began a prolonged series of provocative actions to test the resolve of western democracies. Some of the most successful ones included the installation of puppet Soviet governments in East Germany, Estonia, Lithuania, Latvia, and Czechoslovakia. They coddled pro-Soviet Yugoslavia ruled by communist leaning Tito. The Berlin Airlift and the successful implementation of the Marshall Plan saved most of Western Europe from the same fate. The Dulles brothers were in positions of leadership of both these efforts, and it can be argued that their policies and actions saved some western democracies in Europe and created a new democratic Japan.

But communist successes in Asia included the overthrow of a pro-western government in China, and the US acceptance of communist allied governments in North Korea and North Vietnam. These governments came to power during the postwar era and instituted communist dictatorships in these nations that persist to this day. The United States government had a "hands off" attitude towards these developments during the early post-war period and concentrated their efforts towards rebuilding Western Europe and Japan.

Latin America had been seen for centuries as a safe zone for American interests. The United States viewed the Region as a conglomerate of nations where the US was in a leadership position and where the archaic Monroe doctrine[40] was supposed to provide a safety net to keep out foreign players from interfering with their

---

[40] Monroe Doctrine – James Monroe – fifth president of the United States – Buried in a routine annual message delivered to Congress by President James Monroe in December 1823, the doctrine warned European nations that the United States would not tolerate further colonization or puppet monarchs in the Americas

political affairs. These countries located in Central America, South America and the Caribbean, constituted the **largest** bloc of buyers of American Products in the world. This mind set was strongly held by American intellectuals, industrialists, leaders in Academia and politicians. Unfortunately this belief evolved into a paternalistic attitude towards Latin American leaders and a disastrous foreign policy in the region that persists to this day.

In the waning years of Eisenhower's second term, many members of the US intelligence community began to suspect that the Soviet Union and the communist international movement[41] had set their sights on Cuba as a beachhead for communist penetration into the Latin American family of nations. They were right.

Dick Bissell and the Cuba Special Group

Image 22: *Richard M Bissell Jr. Deputy Director Planning - CIA*

---

[41] Communist International – successor to the Comintern established In 1919 by V. Lenin, it has mutated under his successors. It was essentially an organized attempt by the Soviet Union to control communist parties in other nations.

The CIA operated a Special Organization known as the 5412 Group[42] that had responsibility for implementing all covert actions required to implement key policy initiatives. To handle the tasks necessary to remove Castro from power, a special subgroup was created by Allen Dulles during the Eisenhower administration. This ad-hoc group was referred to as the Cuba group. This special group was placed under the direct leadership of Richard Bissell – D/DP (Deputy Director of Planning).

Cuban affairs in the CIA were routinely handled by Branch 4 of the DD/P Western Hemisphere Division. This Division was headed by Colonel Joseph. C. King, a West Point graduate. The Cuba Group was under the Deputy Director of Planning, creating a conflict of leadership. To complicate matters, air operations which turned out to be a critical area of the activities of this group, were under the control of another CIA organization led by General Charles Cabel, also a West Point graduate and WWII veteran. He was Deputy Director of Central Intelligence (not a part of the DD/P Group) and he did not like to collaborate with other agency groups.

Bissel's other deputies and peers that planned the operations of the Cuba group and carried out much of the daily oversight and decision making were:

C. Tracy Barns Assistant Deputy Director of Planning – Education Groton – Yale – Harvard Law School - WWII Air Force Intelligence Officer – CIA career officer

---

[42] NSC 5412/2 – National Security Council enabling resolution 5412-2 - Designated representatives of the Secretary of State and of the Secretary of Defense of the rank of Assistant Secretary or above, and a representative of the President designated for this purpose, shall hereafter be advised in advance of major covert programs initiated by CIA under this policy or as otherwise directed, and shall be the normal channel for giving policy approval for such programs as well as for securing coordination of support therefore among the Departments of State and Defense and the CIA

Jacob Esterline – Chief Western Hemisphere Branch 4 (Cuba) – Education – Temple University – WWII OSS officer – commanded guerrilla units in India / Burma – CIA career officer

In 1960 the DOD assigned Colonel Jack Hawkins USMC as chief paramilitary officer to assist the group with the landing aspect of the invasion. Much of his sound advice was ignored. This was a CIA operation and the DOD was to be kept out of it.

You will note that **none** of these CIA decision makers planning the Cuban operations had any previous direct experience with Cuba and had no experience in planning large-scale military operations. They tried to apply the experiences of engineering a successful coup in Guatemala to overthrowing the Cuban government – Guatemala and Cuba at that time were two very different places.

In hindsight it seems to me that the final recommendation that the President give the go ahead order to a plan that President Kennedy had extensively modified and weakened to the point where it could not possibly succeed was a huge error in judgement and validates the concept that "military operations should be planned, administered and executed by qualified military officers, not by bureaucrats or political appointees".

CIA Cuba Group Strategies

The initial activities of the Cuba group were focused on recruiting Cuban nationals who met the requirements for paramilitary activity. The CIA focused on providing them with the training needed to use espionage skills they would need to survive in Cuba while building a clandestine network of resistance fighters.

These groups were known as Teams de Infiltración [43] and training was initially provided in the Florida Everglades. In 1960, the CIA built a training facility on Useppa Island, a remote largely uninhabited key in Lee County Florida, near Fort Myers for this purpose. A large number of brave young Cubans risked their life, and

---

[43] Teams de Infiltración – Infiltration Teams

many paid the ultimate price, by being inserted into Cuba and trying to set up underground cells to coordinate the uprising against Castro when the invasion came. They received little or no support from their sponsors. Many of these lives were lost, along with the lives of people who joined these cells because of the fear the CIA had that the Cubans would compromise the US if overt support was provided.

The entire operation was undertaken under a policy of "plausible deniability" which US politicians continued to use in future CIA operations in Vietnam and elsewhere.

Kennedy Administration Relationship with Cuban Exiles

Image 23: *Manuel Artime, José San Román, Antonio Maceo and Tony Varona in Guatemala 1960*

One of the most evident and huge disconnects between the CIA leadership and the anti-Castro people of Cuba whom they were trying to help, was their relationship with the Cuban exile community and more importantly with the Cuban underground, the "clandestinaje". The CIA's culture at that time required complete secrecy regarding operational plans and rejected input from the field as untrustworthy. Many of the resupply missions flown from Guatemala to aid rebel forces on the ground prior to the actual invasion wound up in enemy hands due to this lack of coordination with the Cuban counter revolution.

An interesting aside – recruited at the early stages were a disproportionately large number of young men who had studied or graduated from Cuban Catholic High Schools, from the Colegio de la Salle del Vedado (my alma mater) I can think of five who were in the same promotions as my brother and I – Mario and Jorge Silva, Rafael Montalvo, Humberto Díaz Argüelles, and José Ignacio Smith.

The final tally provided by Billy Muir of the Bay of Pigs Veteran Association:

> Colegio de Belén (Jesuits) – 117
> Colegio de la Salle (Christian Brothers) - 39.

La Salle still holds the moral edge; Fidel Castro graduated from Belén, not from La Salle…

Although there were many young people from Catholic schools, the personnel of the Brigade reflected the diversity of the Cuban people as well as represented all socioeconomic backgrounds.

Recruiting Brigade Members in the US

During the second half of 1959 the Cuban exile population increased dramatically in the United States. As planning continued at the CIA, the agency set up a covert operation aimed at recruiting young capable Cuban exiles to staff the infiltration teams and the planned assault group for the invasion of Cuba. They sent several field agents to Florida and Panama to set up dummy corporations to handle logistics. The Cuba project CIA team then coordinated with the Navy for the use of facilities at the Old Naval Air Station in the Opa Locka Airport and leased facilities at Useppa Key off Florida's west coast, to train the newly recruited members.

My brother and I met several of these agents in Miami. I remember meeting a person who called himself Frank.

Frank had an interesting background. His real name was Frank Angelo Fiorini; he had been a Marine in the Pacific theater in WWII, served under Col "Red" Mike Merritt Edison and was trained by the OSS. He was discharged but joined the US Navy Reserve and the United States Army in the post-war era, serving in Berlin during the Berlin Airlift crisis. He then went to Cuba and joined Fidel Castro's 26 de Julio guerrilla force. After the revolution he was part of the firing squad that killed 71 former Batista supporters in San Juan Hill near Santiago de Cuba. He became disillusioned with the revolution after he realized that many of the top leaders were communists.

Image 24: *Comandante Pedro Luis Díaz Lanz*

He left Cuba with Pedro Luis Díaz Lanz, chief of the FAR (Cuban Revolutionary Air Force). The group had hijacked a small boat and crossed the Florida Straits with Díaz Lanz's family and another Cuban Air Force officer.[44] He was immediately contacted by the CIA and asked to work on the Cuba project. Díaz Lanz was not offered to play a leadership role in the Brigade Air Force when it was formed in Guatemala and instead joined Operacion 40 – a Cuban exile group that conducted several CIA financed operations against the Cuban regime[45].

Frank's primary job was to talk to prominent Cuban exile leaders and to convince them that the full support of the United States would be provided to bring about the removal of Castro and the implementation of the original goals of the revolution: Return to democracy and the rule of law under Cuba's 1940 Constitution. Every Cuban exile in the US believed in this pledge with religious fervor and gave the CIA their full support.

There were several opposition exile groups in Miami at that time. The most well known was the Movimiento de Recuperación Revolucionaria (MRR)[46]. Their leader was Manuel Artime who was the leader of the MRR and later became the Brigade's political representative. Other popular leaders in Miami at that time were Nino Díaz who had been an active Comandante [47] in the Sierra Maestra mountains and Operación 40 with Pedro Luis Díaz Lans, who had been chief of the FAR (Revolutionary Air Force). There were wild rumors that he had flown one of their B-26 aircraft to Miami (not true).

---

[44] United States Department of State - FOREIGN RELATIONS OF THE UNITED STATES, 1958–1960, CUBA, VOLUME VI

[45] Spartacus Educational Website – American History – Operation 40

[46] MRR – Movimiento de Recuperación Revolucionaria – Movement for Revolutionary Recuperation –founded by Comandante Nino Díaz and led by Manuel Artime – ex members of the 26th of July movement who defected in 1959 due to ideological clashes with the Castro brothers and who later joined the Assault Brigade 2506. Nino Díaz commanded one of the planned invasion groups and Manuel Artimes was the Brigade's political officer

[47] Comandante – Literally meant Major but in reality was the top rank given to a guerrilla leader – it was initially the highest rank in the Ejército Rebelde (Rebel Army).

There were Cuban exiles in other parts of the US (New York, New Jersey, Chicago, Los Angeles) and many in Spain, Mexico and Venezuela.

Artime's MRR provided some of the first Cuban agents recruited and trained by the CIA in Useppa Key, whose mission was to infiltrate into Cuba and assist the Cuban resistance with the resupply of their cells and conducting sabotage operations.

I remember spending one night sleeping on the floor of a safe house in Miami used by the MRR, waiting for the group to be transported to a training camp to become guerrillas fighting against Castro. Thank God that did not happen; the casualty rate for counter revolutionary guerrillas fighting the revolution was close to 100 %.

Why would a perfectly sane 19 year old (me) consider joining a group of people whom he had just met, who were looking for cannon fodder, so they could launch a revolution against a communist guerrilla leader? I have asked myself this question many times and cannot come up with a reasonable answer. There were two variables that probably tipped the scales: I was 19 years old, the age at which adventure looks like a worthwhile thing, the second was my brother Armando. We were very close and I, being the older brother, firmly believed it was my duty to protect him from the consequences of the many questionable moves he had already done and from making even worse ones in the future.

The real reason was that it was the right thing to do. We had to fight communism and liberate our homeland from the terrible ordeal it was experiencing. It is the same primary motive that inspired most of the 1500 young people that joined and fought in the Brigade.

EL ESCAMBRAY

Image 25: *Some of the Cuban anticommunist forces that fought Castro and his Soviet advisors in the Escambray Mountains 1960-1965*

While the United States was busy recruiting Cuban exiles in the United States, thousands of Cubans, some who had fought against Batista and many more from all walks of life who were totally opposed to the increasingly totalitarian policies of the revolution, joined the counter revolutionary movements, known in Cuba as "el clandestinaje"[48]

Many fought in the streets of Cuban cities, many in the mountains of Oriente Province, but the biggest uprising was in the Escambray Mountains in South Central Cuba. A region that saw many skirmishes against the Batista forces, now became the center of anti-Castro rebellion.

The CIA in its post-mortem review of the Bay of Pigs operation, identified the false assumption that many thousands of Cubans

---

[48] El Clandestinaje – the clandestine movement

would join the Brigade after it landed and defeat the Castro armed forces as one of the primary causes of the failure. They never understood the real causes for the failure of this assumption:

- The extent of the role the Soviet Union and their proxies, the international communist party, played in this struggle.
- Their failure (the CIA's) to adequately support the counter revolution in Cuba.
- The extent, ruthlessness and efficacy of Castro's Secret Police network in **eliminating** dissenters

I did not play a direct part in the struggle of these heroic men and women[49] most of whom paid for their patriotism with their lives. I will tell my wife's family story as a representative example of the actions of thousands of Cuban families and the motivations of many that joined the counter revolution in a tragic and failed effort to topple tyranny. The narrators are my brother in law, Luis Celorio, a teenager at the time, his father Raúl, his son Raulito, and my wife and sister in law Margarita and Julita. They are all material witnesses to the events involving the Celorio family during the fateful months of January through April, 1961

Raúl Celorio's Story

Raúl Celorio y de Sena was an outstanding person. His father, Benito, was a successful attorney who represented the Royal Bank of Canada's interest in Cuba. Benito Celorio married Julieta de Sena, a beautiful and very religious member of one of Cuba's most prominent families. They were instrumental in building the Colegio de Belén, a fantastic Jesuit High School whom you have

---

[49] Many women were active in this struggle and paid with their lives or long prison sentences – notable among them are: Zoila Almeida – la Niña de Placetas, Oristela López, Vivian de Castro and Gloria Agudín.

already met in this story. Raúl and his brothers all attended Belén. So did Fidel Castro. Raúl Celorio was an excellent student and graduated as the Brigadier[50] of his class.

Image 26: *Raúl and Margot Celorio – 1935*

Like most teens in his class, Raúl was faced with the fact that when he graduated, the Universidad de La Habana was closed due to political turmoil in the mid thirties. That did not stop him, he

---

[50] Brigadier de Belén – The school awarded this title to the top student in the graduating class. It was a high honor and very difficult to achieve since academics was only one of the criteria.

enrolled in the University and studied engineering "por la libre"[51] He passed all his courses while working full time as an agronomist in one of his family's tomato farms in the Province of Las Villas. Immediately after graduating he married Carmen Margarita Alonso (Margot), the love of his life and his girlfriend of over six years.

Raúl's family inherited the ownership and administration of the aqueduct in Sancti Spiritus. This was a charter granted to the family when Cuba was still a Spanish colony. The current administrator regarded Raúl as the most appropriate member of the family to succeed him in his position. Raúl regarded this appointment as a sacred trust since the proceeds of the business was one of the principal sources of revenue for his grandmother's extensive family. He settled down to the task of modernizing the aqueduct, replaced the machinery in the pumping station and replaced most of the pipes that brought water to this growing community. This was a long term project; he was constantly modernizing the plant and the process and paid a great deal of attention and money to the chemistry involved in purifying the Río Yayabo's water that eventually would wind up in his hometown's homes and to the modernization of the of the waterwork's distribution system of pipes.

An important part of Raúl and Margot's life was to assist the Catholic Church in providing charitable support to many orphanages, schools for indigent children and the social work done by the nuns and priests of the Diocese of Sancti Spiritus.

A true Christian, his charitable work started at home, with his family and employees. He employed many people in different capacities. One example that will play a key part in our narrative, is his treatment towards the people employed in his household. Luis had a nanny nicknamed Hachita; when Hachita got married Mar-

---

[51] "estudiar por la libre" – The University allowed students who could not attend classes to sit for final exams. If they passed the exams and met graduation requirements, they could earn the desired degree.

got, Raúl's wife, bought her all her wedding clothes, plate servings, linen, etc. She left their employment after that. We will meet her family later on in our story.

Raúl was friends with Mr. Clemens, a Swiss businessman who was the director of the Nestle Food Manufacturing plant in Sancti Spiritus. He secretly arranged for Nestle to provide milk and other Nestle products manufactured there to the various Catholic religious orders that were helping the destitute. The Salesian sisters who ran the Apostolado school my wife and her sister attended, handled the distribution of this aid.

Celorio Children

Image 27: *Celorio Family - My future wife Margarita on the sofa far right - brother Raulito next to his father Raúl – sister Julia sofa far left – brother Luis on the floor - mother Margot on the sofa center.*

The Revolution Comes to Sancti Spiritus

In the fall of 1959 the anti-Batista rebel forces in the Escambray Mountains mounted an offensive against urban areas in the Province of Las Villas. They captured the City of Sancti Spiritus in late November and the rebel forces came to the aqueduct. In command of that group was a Captain of the Ejército Rebelde[52]. He was Hachita's brother[53]. He wrote a document that specified that no harm was to be done to Mr. Celorio, to the aqueduct, and that no one should intervene (steal) Mr. Celorio's car.

January 1st 1959 was a watershed day for all Cubans. The Batista government collapsed and a new charismatic leader stepped into the political void promising a total change in Cuba's society and an end to all of the country's problems (real and perceived). In Sancti Spiritus, like in most Cuban Cities, the new revolutionary mob took power and began to harass the people that were in political power, the former professional military and police, religious leaders and most of all, successful business people.

Raúl was targeted immediately because he checked the boxes for many of these criteria

Their house was spared due to the document given to him by Hachita's brother.

But they could not evade communist persecution. The party leaders began to harass him and other members of the Sancti Spiritus religious and business community on a regular basis.

Luis recalls three such incidents

Raúl belonged to the Caballeros Católicos[54] They were having a meeting in the Iglesia Mayor[55] when the G2[56] came in and de-

---

[52] Rebel Army

[53] You will recall that Hachita worked for the Celorio's

[54] Caballeros Catolicos – A religious organization of catholic men dedicated to charity and social work

tained everyone in the church. They were held there for 6 hours while each person was interrogated. They were warned that they belonged to a counter revolutionary organization (the Catholic Church) and that they and their families would be closely watched.

The second time occurred during a patriotic mass held at the Iglesia de la Caridad. The militia came in and arrested everyone in the Church including the officiating priest and clergy. They held everyone prisoners overnight in the church and released them the next morning after warning them that they had been identified as counter revolutionaries.

The third time was for real. Luis, who was 13 at the time, recalls vividly.

The G2 showed up in the middle of the night, forced the door and came into the house. They had to go by his room to get to his parent's bedroom. He came out of his room to see what was going on.

Are you Raulito Celorio?

No, I am his brother Luis.

They went into my parent's bedroom and arrested my father. When they took him away my mother lost it and started crying and would not stop. She called our cousin Nena who lived very near our home and told her they had taken Raúl away. She came over right away and spent the night with her trying to calm her down.

Raúl was kept as a prisoner in the Topes de Collante Sanatorio in the Escambray Mountains for three months. The Sanatorio, a former hospital for Tuberculosis patients, was now used as a prison for political prisoners and captured suspected counter revolution-

---

[55] Sancti Spiritus had two catholic churches, The Iglesia Mayor was the most prominent and the center of the diocese, La Iglesia de la Caridad, was a parochial church.

[56] G2 – The Rebel Army's department for military intelligence initially used the US Army designation of G2

aries. When he was released he weighed 80 pounds. He was taken to the door of the Sanatorio and told to walk home to Sancti Spiritus (85 kms away through a very mountainous region). In his condition it was pretty certain he would not make it.

He started walking, after an hour a jeep pulled up, it was a militiaman from his home town whom his wife had helped many times. He recognized him, asked him to get in and drove him home.

Leaving Home

In mid April 1961 the political situation was deteriorating rapidly. The G2 and the committees for the defense of the revolution were turning people in and arrests and disappearances increased exponentially. One morning Raúl received a phone call from a friend in the clandestinaje: "they are going to arrest you soon". Raúl decided right there that they had to leave. They got into their car and they pulled Luisito out of school, bought him a shirt so he would not be dressed in his La Salle uniform and took off for La Habana. In the car were the family chauffeur Efraín, Raúl, Margot and Luisito.

As they left Sancti Spiritus they had to pass a checkpoint. It was manned by very young kids in the militia and they were joking around and gave them no trouble. The Central Highway between Sancti Spiritus and La Habana passes through many little towns. There was a checkpoint in every one of them. They were able to go through two more checkpoints but in the last one, the miliciano[57] in charge told them:

"Sir I do not know who you are but you will not be able to pass the next checkpoint"

When they reached the next town (Cabaiguán), Efraín, the chauffeur, told Raúl that he could not go any farther, he had a family

---

[57] Miliciano – militiaman

and he was afraid they would arrest him, and then what would become of his wife and children

Raúl told him:

"Take the car and go back to Sancti Spiritus, you can keep the car until I get back"

Raúl, Margot and Luisito got out of the car and bought a bus ticket to La Habana on the Ranchuelera bus line.

Raúl to Ticket Seller:

"I want to buy 3 tickets to La Habana"

Ticket Seller to Raúl:

Names?

Raúl: "Raúl, Carmen y Luis"

When the bus was ready to go the ticket seller called out; Passengers Raúl, Carmen y Luis you can board.

This was the first time Luisito had heard his mother addressed as Carmen (it was her legal first name); she always was addressed by her nickname Margot.

By the grace of God and the recommendation of that unknown militiaman they made it to La Habana that day.

Los Bandidos del Escambray[58]

During the early months of 1960 many of the rebel forces that had fought against Batista were marginalized or persecuted for their anti-communist beliefs or because they belonged to the middle or upper classes. An increasingly large number went back to the Es-

---

[58] The Cuban press, who was a front for the government, liked to denigrate those who opposed the revolution. The "Bandidos" were in reality a group of farmers, university students, even some high school students as you will see.

cambray where they had fought before and started a new rebellion against the increasingly tyrannical Castro government.

Image 28: *Capture was followed by quick execution – no prisoners were taken*

In 1960 Fidel Castro had made a deal with the Soviet Union regarding the increased level of insurrection in rural areas. The Soviets would send many "specialists", mostly KGB officers, in command of close to 500 Soviet Special Forces troops to plan and lead a military campaign to wipe out the Escambray uprising. This operation is known in Cuban military history as "La Lucha Contra Bandidos"[59]. The Soviet advisors arrived in early 1961 and set up their headquarters in Trinidad, the closest Cuban city to the Escambray Mountains. They directed the Cuban military effort that involved 70,000 regular Revolutionary Army Troops and 110,000 Milicianos (Cuban militia armed forces). Leading the Cuban military forces were Comandantes Raúl Menendez Tomassevich, a founding member of the Cuban Communist Party and Lizardo Proenza. In addition they were assisted by Spanish-Soviet advisor Francisco Ciutat de Miguel, who was also present at the Bay of Pigs Invasion, and who had fought with the communists against Franco in the Spanish Civil War.

---

[59] Lucha contra los bandidos – struggle against the bandits

In return, The Soviet Union would have an increased role in the training and control of Cuban military forces which would be used later on for "wars of national liberation" in other countries where the Soviets were trying to increase their influence.

Image 29: *Castro and Soviet Forces Executing Cuban Patriots in the Escambray Mountains 1961*

Raulito's Story

Raúl's oldest son, Raúl Jr. (nicknamed Raulito) went to the La Salle High School in Sancti Spiritus. Many of his friends in school had strong anti-communist feelings and were in contact with young people who were fighting the government in the Escambray mountains. Some of them were in contact with the underground counter revolution movement in Sancti Spiritus.

They were asked by the underground to take a shortwave radio transmitter and receiver to the rebels. Raulito and one of his classmates agreed to do it.

They set out to make the long trip (85 kms) and asked a friend to take them to Trinidad where they could meet their contact, a member of the resistance that would get them into the mountains.

Fighting in the Escambray

Raulito and his friend were able to deliver their radio and joined a group of rebels. They did not have modern weapons and spent most of their time running away from the increasingly larger number of militia and regular army patrols looking for them. Castro's forces developed a technique they used later in the Bay of Pigs. They would encircle an area they knew was key to the rebels, drove away all local campesinos, burned their crops and waited for the enemy to show up looking for food or water.

Raulito participated in one skirmish. The head of the anti-castro rebel group after the battle told all the high school students to go home, they had no military training and would surely get killed. Raulito and his friend from La Salle started to walk home.

Days later they both were able to reach Sancti Spiritus. Raúl called the parents of Raulito's best friend and in a meeting in his house told them to get their son out of town immediately. Unfortunately they did not listen to him. Days later the G2 knocked on their door, their son was arrested and executed.

Raúl arranged for Raulito to go to La Habana where he went into hiding at the house of his maternal uncle Eustaquio Alonso (nicknamed Junior).

One of the leaders of the clandestinaje in La Habana code named Francisquito, went to Raulito's grandmother's house and spoke to my wife Margarita to find out where he was. He went to Junior's house and took Raulito to the Venezuelan embassy where he was able to obtain asylum. He was granted a student visa by the Venezuelan government, obtained by his uncle Mario who was in exile in Venezuela and vouched for him. Raulito was able to leave Cuba via KLM for Venezuela where he asked for political asylum.

Francisquito, the resistance leader in La Habana, was captured in April 1961 and executed.

The Girls Leave Cuba

In early March Raúl Celorio had a decision to make. He knew that the G2 was arresting the young daughters of suspected counter revolutionaries in Sancti Spiritus, would rape them and use them as pawns to obtain information on opposition cells. He decided to send the girls to Matanzas to live with their uncle Arturo Puentes and his wife Marcelina Alonso.

Monday April 17, 1961. My future wife, Margarita Celorio and her sister Julia were on a bus traveling from the city of Matanzas to the capital of La Habana. Their godparents felt that harboring the girls would raise suspicion from the secret police so they sent them to stay with their grandparents in La Habana. During the trip they witnessed thousands of military vehicles and troop transports headed the opposite way. My wife commented to her sister: "Los que vengan a invadir, los veo muy mal"[60] She had no way of knowing that her future husband was part of the invasion, along with her first cousin, William (Billy) Muir and another first cousin's husband, Enrique (Kiko) Saavedra.

One month after the Bay of Pigs invasion failed, Raúl received a call from the Salesian sisters whom he had often helped in their efforts to assist poor people. The sisters told him that they were going to be expelled from Cuba and would he consider allowing his two daughters to join the sisters and other girls in similar situations on their trip into exile in the United States.

Raúl agreed and thanked them from the bottom of his heart. The nuns then arranged for my future wife and her sister to leave Cuba, disguised as novices, with a group of nuns and other students on the ferry that still operated between La Habana and Key West. In late May 1961 my wife and her sister arrived at the Salesian School, Mary Help of Christians in Patterson, New Jersey. She

---

[60] "Los que vengan a invadir, los veo muy mal" – Whoever is coming to invade is going to be in real bad shape

soon found herself working in nearby factories building toys and bomb detonators.

Image 30: *Headline in Guatemalan newspaper Prensa Libre reporting on expulsion of 136 Catholic priests from Cuba who refused to pledge fealty to communist government*

Escambray Epilogue

The revolt against Castro in the Escambray Mountains raged on from 1960 to 1963 when the Soviet plan ultimately succeeded. It is estimated (no one will ever really know) that between 18 and 20,000 Cuban men, women and children were executed during the "Lucha Contra Bandidos". The farms and dwellings with the belongings of all Cuban guajiros that lived in that region were burned and destroyed.

The Soviets learned a lesson from fighting the Germans, never keep records of your executions.....

GUATEMALA

Image 31: *Flight Line of C-46 and C-54 aircraft used by the Brigade's Air Force at Base Trax, Retalhuleu, Guatemala*

During the fall of 1960 I was very busy with my freshman year Civil Engineering courses at UM. Calculus and Drafting were the hard ones. I had to take a course in learning to use a slide rule. I still have my K&E beauty, the only tangible evidence that I was once an engineering college student. One day my brother who was a senior in high school at that time, came into our room and told me that he and two other friends had volunteered with the CIA to join a military unit that was going to liberate Cuba. I told him that he was crazy but if he was going to go through with this I would go with him.

We left home without saying goodbye to our parents and went to pick up Eddy Lambert and Raúl Vicens, two friends who were going in with us. I distinctly remember "el cieguito"[61] (Raúl) was in the bathroom and we had to wait until he finished. No one told their parents what we were doing. We went from Raúl's home to this house the Frente[62] had in the section of Miami nicknamed

---

[61] "el cieguito" Raúl Vicens wore very heavy glasses at all times, thus his nickname was "the little blind one"

[62] El Frente – The Political Arm of the Brigade was the Frente Revolucionario Democratico. The FRD was a coalition of several anti-Castro groups which was organized in New York in early 1960 and publicly announced at a press

Calle Ocho[63]. There were a number of people seated behind tables in what was once the living room. They asked us many questions regarding our backgrounds, families, activities in Cuba, political leanings etc. I guess all four of us fit their criteria because my brother was assigned serial number 3211, I was serial number 3212.

After a long wait, we were driven to the Opa Locka Naval Reserve air base where we boarded an unmarked C-54 with a group of people we did not know and taxied down the runway on our way to Guatemala. We did not know where we were going. The plane had been sanitized (no markings) and the plane's windows were covered with cardboard taped to the fuselage.

After a very long flight we walked off the plane to a recently built air field named Base Trax in "scenic" Retalhuleu, a province of Guatemala; this Base served as the home of the Brigade 2506 airforce and also as a training facility for the Brigade troops. It was built by the CIA in a coffee plantation belonging to Roberto (Bobby) Alejos who was a close friend of President Ydigoras and had been the Guatemalan Ambassador to the United States. We were given a choice to further volunteer to be part of the Brigade's Airborne Battalion[64]. I was the first to volunteer, all four of us went into the paratroopers.

---

conference in Mexico City on June 21, 1960. The groups composing the FRD were anti-Castro, anti-Communist, and anti-Batista.

[63] Calle Ocho – At the beginning of the Cuban exile in Miami, most Cubans settled in a poor Miami neighborhood surrounding 8th Street SW – in Cuban slang – la Calle Ocho or "la Sauwesera"

[64] The Brigade land forces that actually landed in Cuba in 1961 were composed of one airborne unit, six infantry units, a heavy weapons unit, a UDT unit, and a headquarters unit. The actual troop strength totaled 1,500 men – roughly the equivalent of two US Battalions. The units were trained to absorb many additional men who would defect from Castro's armed forces in order to gain full strength staffing. There were additional military units who participated in the invasion but did not land; they included the Brigade's Air Force and Naval units, several reserve troop units in the US and the group led by Nino Díaz who aborted two landings in Oriente province (easternmost end of the island).

Paratroopers

Image 32: *First Airborne Battalion Practice Jump – Quetzaltenango Guatemala*

Sometime in mid November the 1st Battalion (Airborne) was moved to another training facility near Quetzaltenango (a nearby town). The facility consisted of a clearing in the middle of the jungle where tents were erected and some training aids were brought in to familiarize us with the procedure to follow when jumping from a prop aircraft through a side door. We called this base "garrapatenango" (the word garrapata means the parasite tick in Spanish)

Our instructor was a regular army soldier attached to the CIA, he was a WWII vet and he told me that he had taken part in the Normandy invasion. He was to be called by his first name (it was a cover name) and he did not fraternize with the troops. Since I spoke English fluidly I also learned over time that he had recently been in Vietnam as an advisor training French troops. At that time I had no idea what US troops were doing in Vietnam. It was not in the daily news in the States.

We had a dummy wooden aircraft fuselage in camp. You would wear your jump training gear consisting of a training parachute harness with a static line, your plastic jump helmet (in reality they were football helmets), your weapon and ammo and your boots. We would sit on the training fuselage and the PDO[65] would go through the drill:

Stand Up!

Hook Up!

Check your equipment! (you checked your gear and the gear of the trooper next to you)

Check your static line! (it had to slide freely on a cable installed in the middle of the cabin so it would open your main chute when you jumped)

First squad to the door!

Jump!!!

When you hit the dirt you had to do a PLF[66] We did this over and over until the instructor was satisfied (they usually were not).

We moved on to the static jump from an approximate 20 meter high wooden platform where the fall and landing portion were simulated by jumping attached to a cable that retarded your fall speed. This exercise was supposed to give you an initial feel of what would happen in an actual jump but it was not even close…

---

[65] PDO – Parachute drop officer – a member of the Brigade Air Force whose job it was to help get the airborne unit to jump over the designated LZ (landing zone)

[66] PLF – Parachute landing fall – designated way to fall on the ground to prevent broken bones or other injuries. You had to roll on your non-weapon side (I had a BAR so I was not very flexible), then get up and immediately remove your chute harness so you would not be dragged if the wind picked up.

Other segments of the training consisted of firing our weapons, hand to hand combat including combat knife, 45 caliber pistol and use of explosives, primarily our hand grenades and C-4 for structure demolition; and running – running – running everywhere and all the time…..

When going to bed at the end of a long day we slept in a sleeping bag in a field cot. When waking up you checked your boots to make sure a "Niño Dormido"[67], scorpion or other bug had not crawled into your boots while you slept.

Regular hygiene included bathing in your skivvies in a stream that had a waterfall near the camp. It felt like heaven to get the filth off you and having a few moments of peace and quiet.

The big day finally came when we crawled in the back of an army truck and drove back to Base Trax. I remember this vividly.

We marched into this big hangar where we were issued our chutes. Like the rest of our gear we used WW2 surplus T10/T2 parachutes[68]. They were packed by our advisors at the Trax base. We helped each other to put them on and made sure you were strapped in properly. Then we sat and looked at the Curtiss C-46 that was going to take us on our first training jump. I remember clearly sitting on the hangar floor and thinking out loud: "Are you suuure you want to get into that perfectly good airplane and jump out the door???" It did not seem very logical to me at that time

Finally we all lined up and boarded. It was a short flight to the LZ.

---

[67] Niño Dormido – a type of coral snake that was highly venomous – would paralyze your heart in 4 seconds after venom reaching your heart. – it loved warm closed spaces like our boots.

[68] The T-10 Parachute is a static line-deployed parachute used by the United States armed forces for combat mass-assault airborne operations and training. The average rate of descent is from 22 to 24 feet per second (6.7 to 7.3 m/s); total suspended weight limitation is 360 pounds (160 kg). The parachute is deployed using either a 15 or 20 feet (4.6 or 6.1 m) static line. We jumped from 1200 to 800 ft altitude giving us an average of 25 seconds hang time in the air.

STAND UP, CHECK YOUR EQUIPMENT, CHECK YOUR STATIC LINE, 3^D SQUAD TO THE DOOR, JUMP!!!

You watch the tail of the plane swishh over you, then a big jerk and thankfully your canopy opens, you hug your T2 reserve chute and take in the awesome silence as the ground gets closer and closer, you steer your chute using the risers, try to avoid people and specially trees on the ground and finally you hit the ground. I forgot to do a PLF and scrambled to get out of the harness and collapse the canopy. A fantastic feeling of relief and accomplishment swept over me. I had not chickened out and was on the ground in one piece. Life was good. I went over to look for my brother who was in the same squad and carried the extra ammo for my BAR.

Here is a little incident that actually happened that elevated our instructor to the "can do no wrong status". The paratrooper American advisors made a bet among themselves that they would hold a race. The rules were:

> They would jump in Bermuda shorts and t-shirts
>
> No boots – ours jumped wearing rubber thongs
>
> Each would jump with a bottle of Jack Daniels and the bottle had to be empty when they landed.

They did that one afternoon after we had jumped and assembled to return to camp. We all saw it. We were very impressed...

NICARAGUA

Image 33: *Elements of First Airborne Battalion listening to a briefing by US CIA Advisors – April 16 1961 – Puerto Cabezas Air Base – Nicaragua*

Around the tenth of November 1960 the airborne battalion was transported to Base Trax. We knew something was up since training was over. We were issued our gear (Troopers in Company D had 81 and 60 mm mortars and bazookas and had to jump with a leg or drop bag[69] containing their weapons and ammo) I had an ammo vest to carry BAR 20 round clips of .30-06 caliber ammunition. We were issued these cool Australian style cowboy hats in

---

[69] Drop bag also called GP bag - The drop bag was a reinforced canvas kit bag attached by a canvas detachable strap to the parachute harness and strapped to one of the paratroopers' legs. It usually contained the soldier's additional ammo, any special equipment needed for his mission and his share of the unit's ammunition reserve.

the photo, they did not see a lot of action. We had a bowie knife and a .45 automatic and ammo for that weapon. I also carried a couple of fragmentation grenades. We had a canteen but were not issued any food rations.

On the fifteenth we boarded a C-54 transport and flew to Nicaragua. We had to make an emergency landing since the pilot did not get a green light on the right main landing gear. After asking the tower if they saw that all the gear was down, he came in and eased that sucker down on the left wheel and then touched on the right to see if it would hold. It did and there was a big cheer in the back since we were also carrying a few thousand pounds of ammo and explosives.....

Never knew who the Cuban pilot was, but in my book his name is: "pretty damned good pilot"....

Air Operations – April 15 1961

I cannot provide a firsthand detailed account of the vastly complex air operations conducted over Cuba which started in1960 with paradrops for the insurgents fighting in the Escambray Mountains, in the Central province of Las Villas, and in the Sierra Maestra, Sierra de Nicaro and Sierra de Moa Mountains in the easternmost province of Oriente, culminating with the heroic actions of Cuban and American Advisors flying suicide combat sorties over Girón against Castro's jets and Sea Fury fighters during the invasion.

I will use information published in the excellent book Operación Puma by Captain Eduardo Ferrer, who commanded the transport squadron of the Cuban Liberation Air Force in the Bay of Pigs and who wrote a detailed and very factual account of these operations.

The Cuban pilots decided to adopt the name of Fuerza Aérea de Liberación (Liberation Air Force) and had an incredibly high morale and level of training.

Inventory of Aircraft – Fuerza Aérea Revolucionaria (Castro's Air Force)

Operational Combat Aircraft

5 - Lockheed T-33 Jet Fighter (armed with 2 – 50 cal machine guns and rockets under the wing)

5 – Hawker Sea Fury (4 – 20 mm machine guns, rockets under the wings and bombs)

6 – Douglas B-26 light bombers (6 – 50 cal machine guns on the wing – two rear turrets each armed with 2 – 50 cal machine guns – rockets and bombs)

Operational Support Aircraft

1 - PBY Catalina

Non – Operational Military Aircraft

2 - F-47 fighters

2 – F-51 fighters

Undisclosed number of MIG jet fighters in crates
Several transport aircraft.

Inventory of Operational Combat Aircraft – Fuerza Aérea de Liberación - (Brigade 2506 Air Force)

17 – A-26 light bombers Armament: 8 – 50 cal machine guns in nose, 8 air to ground rockets under the wings and bombs. Modified to remove rear gun turrets and add additional fuel tanks

Operational Support Aircraft

C54 and C46 Transport aircraft

April 15 Air Strikes

The Kennedy policy team finally gave a green light but scaled back and severely curtailed the original plan developed during the Eisenhower Administration. It should be noted that on Kennedy's policy team, Dean Rusk the Secretary of State, was totally opposed to the invasion and insisted on the US adhering to the policy of plausible deniability discussed previously. Also opposed were Adlai Stevenson, Ambassador to the UN, and Theodore Sorensen, Kennedy's speech writer and personal friend. Robert McNamara, Secretary of Defense, was neutral (an interesting position given his job). It is not clear to me how the most important advisor to Jack Kennedy, his brother Bobby who was Attorney General, felt. On April 15 the first of three planned air strikes designed to take out the Castro Air Force and severely limit its ability to defeat the invading forces took place.

The first planned air strike flight plan called for A-26's to strike key targets identified by air reconnaissance flights by the CIA. **On the morning of the 15th the US advisors had to tell the Cuban pilots that the number of planes for this mission had been cut back from 16 to 8.** Consternation followed by questions as to why they did that, and did they not understand that reducing the number of planes in the first wave would eliminate any advantage from the element of surprise. The selected crews swallowed the bitter news and went into their pre-flight routines.

Results of the Air Missions on April 15

Puma Flight – Objective: Ciudad Libertad Airfield, La Habana
Fuerza Aérea Revolucionaria
Planes destroyed : 1 – B26
Ammunition Depot Destroyed
FAR HQ Building: Destroyed
Fuerza Aérea de Liberación
Planes lost to AA fire: 1 A-26

Gorilla Flight – Objective: Antonio Maceo Airport, Santiago de Cuba
FAR Planes destroyed : 1 – Sea Fury 1 – PBY 1 – B-26 1 – C-47
1- Commercial Airline
Several Small Planes
AA Battery Destroyed
Fuerza Aérea de Liberación
Planes lost: None

Linda Flight – Objective: San Antonio de los Baños Airbase – San Antonio de los Baños
FAR Planes destroyed : 1 – T-33 2 – F-47 (not operational) 1 – T-6 Trainer
Partially disabled planes: 2 - B-26
1- AA 37mm cannon Battery Destroyed
Fuerza Aérea de Liberación
Planes lost: None

Castro's Air Force had not been neutralized and still had sufficient strength to defeat the invasion.

April 16

Image 34. Admiral Arleigh Burke – Naval Chief of Staff

If you look at the JFK Presidential Library for a reference for the cancellation of the air strikes planned for April 16 you will see the following explanation:

"The first mishap occurred on April 15, 1961, when eight bombers left Nicaragua to bomb Cuban airfields. The CIA had used obsolete World War II B-26 bombers, and painted them to look like Cuban air force planes. The bombers missed many of their targets and left most of Castro's air force intact. As news broke of the attack, photos of the repainted U.S. planes became public and revealed American support for the invasion. President Kennedy cancelled a second air strike."[70]

This is a bold-faced lie.

The order to conduct a campaign of misinformation to try to convince the world that the planes conducting the strike were Cuban Air force planes flown by defectors came from the White House.

For weeks the CIA and the Chiefs of Staff had advised Kennedy that the changes in the original plan to relocate the site of the invasion, and to negate air support from the American fleet carriers that had been assembled by orders of Navy Chief of Staff Admiral Arleigh Burke, were a **major** mistake that would reduce the probability of success.

Kennedy acted **against the direct advice** from both the CIA and the Chiefs of Staff when he reduced the first airstrike from 16 planes to 8 and cancelled the follow up air strikes planned for April 16th.

On April 16 on learning that Kennedy had given an order to cancel the two follow up airstrikes scheduled for that day, Burke drove to the White House and engaged in a shouting match with the president that ended in a very famous quote. When told by the president that his decision was based on the fact "that he wanted to ensure that the perception would be that no US forces were directly involved in the invasion", Burke replied:

"Goddammit Mr. President, we are involved and there is no way we can hide it, we are involved!!!"

---

[70] John F Kennedy Presidential Library Website – The Bay of Pigs Invasion

Kennedy opted to listen to the politicians and ignore the military's advice.

As the pilots were debriefing for their flights the next day the incredible news of the cancellation of the strikes was announced. The news cast a pall on their celebrations. They swallowed the bitter pill but remained committed to their cause.

The chief American Advisor for the air campaign on site, Air Force General Reid Doster of the Alabama Air National Guard read the wire, shook his head and said:

"There goes the whole fucking war!!!"

The decision to cancel the strikes was made by President Kennedy. He operated under the delusion that it was more important to please the international community and the press, than to achieve key policy objectives. Later he admitted his error when he stated publicly that he alone was responsible for the failure of the invasion.

Paratroopers in Puerto Cabezas – Happy Valley Airbase – April 15-16

We spent the fifteen and sixteen of April watching our A-26's and the Nicaraguan Air Force prop fighters and jets taking off in between briefings by our advisors.[71] Nicaragua provided the airport and the sea port facilities but did not participate in the military operations. We could have used those jets to escort our defenseless A-26's over Girón in the following days but unfortunately they did not have the range or refueling capabilities to provide air support.[72]

---

[71] In 1961 the Nicaraguan Air Force operated a number of P-51 mustangs, F-47 Thunderbolts and AT-33 armed trainer jets.

[72] A-26 Invader was a WW2 era light attack bomber used for ground support in WW2 and Korea. Our planes belonged to the Alabama Air National Guard.

I will try to summarize the principal components for the failure of the Bay of Pigs planning process.

The process was constrained by key decisions made during the planning period by individuals who did not have a proper military background, and who were not qualified to plan, modify or make decisions related to major military operations. These decisions would later lead to failure since the objectives could not be achieved with the equipment and forces provided.

In the briefings by our advisors we received one consistent message – We were going to quickly defeat Castro and be joined by tens of thousands of dissidents and **march triumphantly into La Habana!!!**.

While we were fed this completely erroneous information, the Castro government was busy rounding up anyone that was suspected to be a collaborator with the invaders. People were crammed into theaters, movie houses, baseball stadiums and any other building where they could safely hold prisoners. Only God knows how many people were executed that night, including most of the leadership of the counter revolutionary movement inside Cuba.

We slept on the runway next to our gear. That night we suited up, boarded our C46 and took off for our landing zone. Next stop, the little town of San Blas, on the road between Central Covadonga and Playa Girón. We had to block one of 3 roads providing access to our invasion "beaches" and our primary objective, the airfield in Playa Girón.

One final note, on April 16, the day after he cancelled the follow up air strikes, a decision that doomed the invasion, President Kennedy's schedule notes that he spent the day Playing Golf....

The range of the aircraft was 2,250 kms so they had to be modified to add extra gasoline tanks by removing the rear turret assembly. This had to be done due to the range of the aircraft and the distance from Puerto Cabezas, Nicaragua to Playa Girón, Cuba (927 kms). Flying time over targets in the Girón battlefield was reduced to 10-15 minutes if the pilot wanted to be able to reach Nicaragua on a return flight.

INVASION

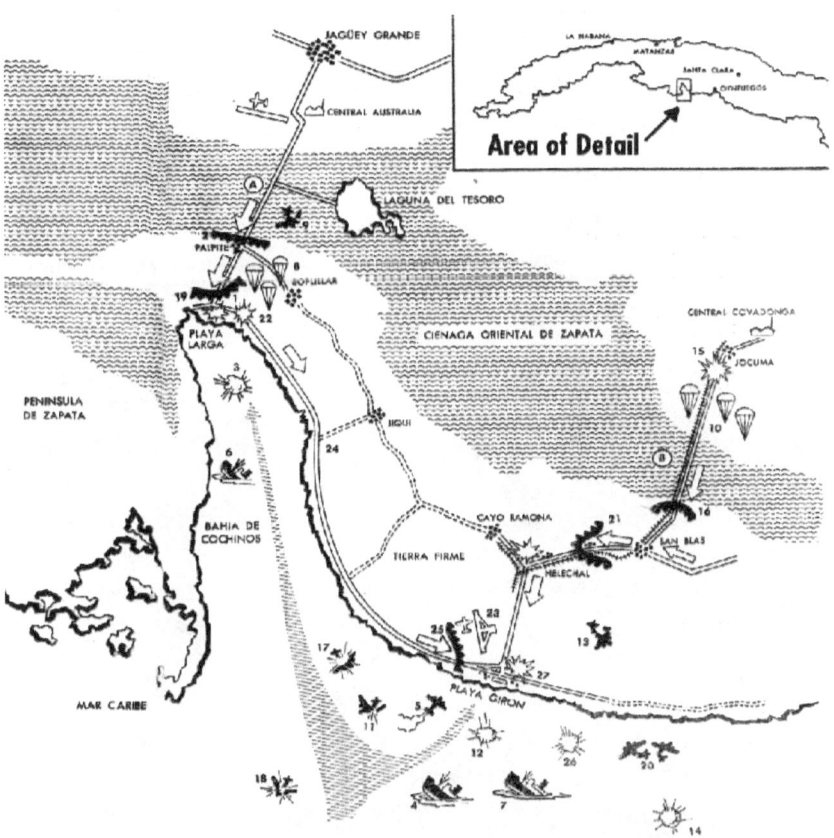

Image 35: *The modified invasion plan included landings at Playa Larga (19), Playa Girón (27). Air Drops LZ's were at Palpite-Soplillar (22) and San Blas (21)*

The Girón site was chosen in part because theoretically it could be easily defended. There were two major two lane roads leading into the area that led to the Carretera Central (Central Highway) at the towns of Jaguey Grande and Aguada de Pasajeros. There were two large sugar cane mills at Central Australia and Central Covadonga. These Sugar Mills were later used by Castro as staging areas and command and control centers for the army, militia, artillery and tank units that were trucked and bused to the battle front.

The problem with this site selection was glaringly obvious. The Playa Girón landing site was very remote and removed from any population center that would provide links to the counter-revolutionary forces. There was no infrastructure there that could be used to the Brigade's advantage. It was also very easy to attack if you had control of the air.

Monday

Image 36: *Satellite Image of the town of San Blas - our squad's LZ is the white circle*

On April 17 the weather was beautiful in the Ciénaga de Zapata[73] I remember standing for a second on the door of the airplane at

---

[73] Ciénaga de Zapata – Zapata Swamp – Cuba's largest (4,350 square kms) The area where we landed is actually mostly pockmarked calcareous rock that re-

around 6:15 am and taking in that beautiful blue Cuban dawn. The Cuban sky never seemed so blue, the weather was perfect. It did not seem real that I was about to jump out of this airplane to save my country from communism!!!

Our drop was picture perfect, we folded and hid the chutes and assembled to take the town of San Blas. The militia defenders had watched the airdrop thinking that we were Ejército Rebelde troops conducting a practice exercise.[74] They surrendered without firing a shot. We took our first prisoners and proceeded to hike north to set up our defensive position. We left a squad back at San Blas to establish liaison with the infantry and heavy weapon units that were landing at Girón Beach at that time and to guard the prisoners.

We hiked about 5 klicks north and set up our defensive position cutting the Covadonga – San Blas Road. Our first objective had been achieved. We sat and waited for the enemy to show up. We didn't have to wait long.

A line of buses appeared on the road and elements of what we learned later were the 117th militia battalion of Cienfuegos[75] attacked with small arms. We were soon reinforced by additional Brigade infantry troops that landed on Red Beach (Playa Girón) and received covering mortar fire from the Heavy Weapons battalion. We were under small arms fire during that day and night but held our position.

On the western front at Playa Larga things were much worse. The paratroopers from Company A that jumped near the small town of Palpite to cut the road from Central Australia, landed under heavy

---

tains water and the vegetation consists of shrubs and very small scrubby trees. There is a very large and beautiful lagoon (Laguna del Tesoro). The Ciénaga was completely undeveloped prior to Castro. Population consisted mostly of carboneros, peasants that made a living burning shrub trunks to make charcoal.

[74] Ejército Rebelde – Rebel Army – this was the name used to refer to the regular Cuban army under Castro.

[75] Militia Battalion – Paramilitary unit consisting of male or female adults who were conscripted in their homes or places of business and given weapons and small arms training

enemy fire with one casualty killed in the descent, Herman Koch. They linked up with the Infantry's second battalion and third battalion as well as elements of the Heavy Weapons Battalion (4.2 inch mortars) and tanks. Unfortunately the Fifth Battalion was not able to land in Playa Larga as planned. Their transport ship, the Houston, was sunk by fighters from Fidel's Revolutionary Airforce (FAR). Most of the Brigade's troops on that ship had to swim to safety on the other side of the bay and were unable to participate in the action. Some, like the husband of my wife's cousin, Enrique Saavedra were able to swim to the Playa Larga beach; this was their designated landing site and they were incorporated into the troops that were setting up the defensive line there.

Enemy column under attack by Liberation Air Force B-26's.

Image 37: *The Battalion of the Policía Nacional Revolucionaria attacked by Brigade's A-26*

Enrique Saavedra's Story

At noon, Enrique remembers walking with one of the 5th Battalion Houston sinking survivors to help set up the defense perimeter on the highway. In the distance he could see many buses which he assumed were full of militia troops. Our A-26's bombed this convoy with napalm explosives and he recalls the cries from the wounded, a sound he will never be able to forget.

The enemy kept bringing on troops to the front, A firefight started that lasted two full days and nights. It kept getting worse with mortars and artillery fire from the Castro forces answered by our mortars and tanks. He thought: this is what hell must look like...

Air Operations – Monday April 17

Image 38. *Sinking of the Houston Opposite Playa Larga - all gasoline and supplies on this ship were lost - most of the infantry troops swam to the wrong side of the bay and never saw combat*

Monday brought another set of disappointing news from Washington. The second planned air strike to destroy Castro's Air Force had been cancelled and replaced with orders to provide air support to the invading forces. Recall that Castro still had several T-33 jets and superior Sea Fury fighter aircrafts operational and ready to go into action.

At 02:45 Monday Linda Flight (2 A-26) took off on a mission to deny Castro naval support. They flew to the Isle of Pines directly South of La Habana and sank the Castro frigate El Baire. This mission was successful.

Linda Flight flew to Girón and joined Lobo flight (2 A-26) to provide air cover for the paratrooper drops. Linda's planes ran out of fuel and headed back to Nicaragua. Lobo ran a bombing / strafing mission at Playa Larga and then flew to the Laguna del Tesoro where they sank a Cuban patrol boat.

At 03:45 Chico flight (2 A-26) left Nicaragua to fly air support. They saw the sinking Houston troop ship and engaged one FAL Sea Fury who was strafing the Rio Escondido troop carrier. They engaged the enemy in a dog fight and were able to damage it and he fled towards his base. Another Sea Fury appeared and they engaged the enemy aircraft and caused him to leave the area. Then a T-33 appeared and strafed one of the A-26's; it tried to land on the Girón Airfield but blew up as it touched down. Incredibly one of our pilots survived the crash.

Two more combat patrols by Gorilla Flight 1 and 2 reached Girón at 09:30 where they saw a T-33 strafing and firing rockets at the Rio Escondido (another Brigade cargo troop ship) which eventually exploded and sank. Gorilla 1 and 2 provided air cover for the Houston which had been beached that morning after taking direct hits from the air.

Another air patrol was flown that morning, code-named Paloma 1 and 2. While performing a strafing run, Paloma 2 took a hit to one of the engines and flew to Grand Cayman Island where he made an emergency landing. Paloma 1 made a strafing pass at the Central Covadonga front and was attacked by a T-33 which seriously damaged our plane, the pilot headed out to the safety zone provided by the US Navy fleet offshore and instructed his copilot to jump at an altitude of 800 feet. He did and was picked up by a Navy destroyer, USS Murray. Unfortunately the plane crashed into the ocean before the pilot could jump. The A-26 was not designed to float; the pilot was drowned.

Lion 1 and Lion 2 followed, Lion 1 had engine trouble and had to fly back to Nicaragua. Lion 2 arrived at Girón for his combat air patrol and was lucky that the Castro fighters had gone back to base. He tried to fly back to Happy Valley low on gas and his plane crashed just miles from the airport. He was listed as missing in action and his plane was not found until a year after the invasion. Both pilots died in the crash.

Image 39: *Lt. Rafael del Pino- of Castro's FAR - flew this T-33 jet*

Rafael del Pino – FAR T-33 pilot shot down 2 of the Brigade's A-26 attack bombers and sank two Brigade naval units. He went on to become Deputy Commanding Officer of Castro's FAR and later defected to the United States.

At 15:05 Puma 1 and Puma 2 arrived over Girón on a combat patrol. They received intelligence from the ground that there was a very large troop convoy on the road headed to the Brigade's Playa Larga defensive position. They proceeded to bomb the convoy and inflicted heavy casualties. Two T-33 jets appeared and Puma 2 radioed his wingman "I have T-33's on my tail, get out of here"

The second T-33 was soon on Puma 1's tail, he knocked out his left engine, but at the last moment a Skyraider from the USS Essex appeared and scared away the T-33 and a Sea Fury that had joined the chase. The Skyraider followed his orders and did not pursue or fire on the Cuban planes. Puma 1 attempted to fly his wounded bird back to base but had to ditch; he and his copilot are listed as missing in action.

One final mission was flown by Captain Ferrer in a C-54 escorted by two A-26's. The objective was to bring in ammunition and gas to the invading troops who had no resupply as their ships had been sunk. The 2 A-26's escorts had to abort, one had engine failure, the other one could not get the machine guns to work. Ferrer flew on anyway, conscious that a C-54 was a sitting duck for any of Castro's fighters. He listened to the exchanges between the pilots in the Puma flight and decided that with fighters in the air he needed to abort the mission to save the aircraft and his crew. No ammunition arrived at Girón that day.

Tuesday

Image 40: *Cuban T-34/85 tank staging near Playa Girón, April 1961*

Our opponents were fully aware of where we landed and of our troop strength. The telephone operator of Central Covadonga had spoken to Fidel Castro personally the prior evening to tell him that "there were reports of bright lights and explosions in Playa Girón that evening (April 17 about 2 am). Fidel had previously mobilized the entire Cuban military and paramilitary[76] forces. We saw previously that on the 15th of April, the Brigade Air Force conducted a pre-invasion air raid on the airfields where they thought the FAL (Cuban Air Force) had their aircraft. Again the information was faulty. Castro's spies in the US and in Latin America had correctly predicted the timing and air power of the invading forces and Castro had dispersed his aircraft.

The first elements of the regular army started to arrive on the Covadonga Road front early Tuesday morning. We saw an increase in heavy weapons fire and the sound of the metralletas[77] was replaced by the distinct sound of the AK47's and the swoosh-boom! of the RPG rockets. We were ordered to retreat that morning to the town of San Blas where we dug in on the drainage ditches parallel to the gravel road leading east-west out of town. I witnessed a parade of Soviet T-34 tanks, old US Sherman Tanks and armored vehicles driving toward our position on the road from the Central Covadonga during the entire morning.

Sometime during the day our squad leader, Henry Rodriguez, asked our squad to go into one of the houses in town to bring back some ammunition since we were running low. We walked through this hell armed only with our 45's since we needed our hands to carry the ammo. Coming back I accidentally squeezed out a shot,

---

[76] The Cuban military consisted of regular army units and militia forces – the CIA estimate in Jan 1961 (way low) was 32,000 regular army, air force and navy, 9,000 armed police and 200 to 300 thousand armed militia In reality the regular army strength was closer to 50,000 men.

[77] Metralletas – militia units were usually armed with submachine guns of East German or Czech origin

Henry turned around and asked me – who the hell are you firing at? – the answer – not at you Cadete[78]

Here is an incident that burned in my memory. Sometime that afternoon a truck with armed men and what looked like a thirty caliber mounted on the roof and fired by a soldier from the open bed drove into the town at high speed spraying bullets all around. There was a concrete roundabout in the intersection of these roads, my brother and I dove behind the cement edge of the roundabout and started firing at the truck. So did a number of other Brigade members around me. I remember thinking – this cement rim is not very high, they can see me clearly from the truck. As the rounds whizzed by, I kept firing until the clip ran out. Then we heard the roar of our M-41 tank as it burst out of the vegetation to my right. I felt sorry for the people in the truck. They didn't make it.

Another mental movie clip – we had a bazooka man whose nickname was "el flaco Valdez"[79] As the tanks threatened to get closer and came into range he would stand on top of a barbed wire fence and brace himself with his legs and the fence post; then he would aim and take a shot, get down, reload, back up the fence and fire again. He was totally exposed for minutes on top of that fence and we were taking all kinds of fire, but he kept doing it. I thought to myself – Coño! Este flaco tiene cojones de acero[80]

Tuesday was a day from hell, but it was nothing compared to Tuesday night. The enemy had rolled in their 122 mm artillery and started to take target practice on the town of San Blas and environs. A shell would come in, you would hear the whistling sound, if it landed close to you, the explosion would physically

---

[78] Henry Rodríguez had been a cadet in the Ejército Rebelde's Escuela de Cadetes (Cuban West Point). He is a dear friend and we wound up spending many years together in Atlanta. He has also written a book about his experiences which I recommend you read.

[79] "el flaco Valdez" – Most Cubans rapidly acquire a nickname and are forever referred to by it. Their real name is forgotten. El flaco means the skinny one.

[80] This skinny guy has steel balls

raise you 2-3 feet off the ground and you would land with a thump on your face. We did not get a lot of sleep that night.

In Playa Larga things were getting really hot, Brigade Forces started to receive heavy fire from the Batallón de la Policía Nacional Revolucionaria[81] that arrived that morning. This unit is known in Castro's Fuerzas Armadas Revolucionarias as the "Batallón de la Muerte"[82]. They took very heavy casualties from our Brigade Units and from strafing and bombing runs by our A-26's. Increasing number of regular army and militia units started arriving at Playa Larga and massing for an attack on Girón. There was a tank battle where the Ejército Rebelde deployed Soviet T-34/85, SU100 anti-tank vehicles and US Sherman Tanks against the Brigade's Walker M-41 Bulldog tanks. Our troops mounted a heroic stand and held off the Castro forces until ammo started getting really low.

At sea Monday and Tuesday were absolute disasters. All three of the cargo ships transporting troops, gasoline, ammo and food were attacked by Castro's remaining air force and two were sunk. The Houston was hit by rockets landing troops on Monday. The Cuban captain of the Houston, Luis Morse, beached the burning hulk so that the surviving crew and brigade members could get off and survive. His son was a member of the brigade and was on board. They both made it to shore.

The Río Escondido, which carried most of the ammo and supplies to re-supply the Brigade, was literally blown out of the water. A third ship, the Caribe was damaged, lost its communication equipment and turned tail to avoid air attacks. The captain was able to sail out of Cuban territorial waters. The captain then turned the ship around on Wednesday after repairs were made but arrived too late to be able to be a factor in the invasion.

---

[81] Batallón de la Policía Nacional Revolucionaria. Combat Battalion of the National Revolutionary Police

[82] Batallón de la Muerte – Death Battalion

The only positive note was the downing of a Castro B-26 by anti-aircraft fire from one of our LCI command ships, the Barbara J.

Air Operations – Tuesday April 18

Image 41: *Brigade Air Force A-26 on a bombing run over targets near Playa Larga*

A combat air patrol of 2 A-26's took off at 00:10 to bomb the air base at San Antonio de los Baños; it was scrubbed due to bad weather obscuring the target.

Intelligence was received from ground troops that a large vehicle formation including tanks was approaching Brigade Outposts on the road from Playa Larga to Girón. Three flights of 2 A-26's were scrambled to meet the threat. For the first time, two American advisors disobeyed orders and flew combat missions. The convoy was destroyed and the Castro forces later acknowledged over 900 casualties. The A-26's were able to return to base.

Three C-54's were assigned a mission to drop urgently needed ammo and supplies over Girón. Some of the packages reached land, but not our troops. More than half were swept out to sea.

Wednesday

That morning we were ordered to retreat to a fork in the road about 1click south of town. I remember we were standing on this clearing and the bullets were whizzing around us. We were walking through a lemon orchard. The fire was so heavy that the orange tree leaves next to me would flick continuously when they were hit. A strange feeling of peace fell over me as I was standing there not shielded by anything. I thought "I must have a very strong Ángel de la Guardia[83] for this to make sense". From that incident I developed a strong devotion to Saint Michael the Archangel, patron saint of policemen and of the US Armed Forces.

A Jeep drove up the road and we captured a Comandante of the Ejército Rebelde, his last name was Duque. He was on a reconnaissance mission to determine our troop strength. He took one look around and he told us: "Ríndanse ahora mismo porque los van a matar a todos"[84]

Alejandro del Valle our battalion commander then showed up and yelled "Los paracaidistas no se retiran!"[85] We started a counterattack and retook the town of San Blas.

Image 42: *VA-34's A4D-2 Skyhawks sortied from Essex (CVS 9) opposite Playa Girón during the Invasion*

---

[83] Guardian Angel
[84] Surrender now, they are going to kill all of you"
[85] Paratroopers do not retreat

In the early afternoon it became clear that the navy Skyhawks from the Essex were not going to intervene. The entire naval fleet outside the Cuban territorial waters consisting of two aircraft carriers, destroyers, cruisers and submarines, did not fire a shot[86]. I was strafed by a FAR Sea Fury and a T-33 on Wednesday. I remember standing next to our radio operator who was trying to establish contact with the US Naval forces, he would try all frequencies on his portable radio and say – we need air support, we are getting killed down here- he listened to one reply and then turned to Néstor Pino, our Company commander and said – they (the Skyhawks) have a no shoot order – I later learned while doing research that the information was provided by Erneido Oliva, second in command in the Brigade from the Batallón de Jefatura[87] to Alejandro del Valle, our Battalion commander.

I ran out of ammunition on Wednesday afternoon. We received orders to retreat to the Beach. On the way there we passed one of our M35 trucks standing in the middle of the road. A plane had scored a direct cannon or rocket hit on the engine, pushing it back into the driver. He was still sitting there holding the wheel. We were strafed by a FAR Sea Fury and I remember standing in the middle of the road looking at this fighter shooting his 20mm cannon at us. My thoughts were along these lines[88]: "coño, estoy en una película de John Wayne….."

Enrique Saavedra remembers the retreat back to Playa Girón. He was walking with his friend Eddy de Las Casas and they suddenly saw one of the FAR's Hawker Sea Fury fighters strafing the road. They dove into one of the concrete block houses. His friend Eddy took a 20 mm shell to the head and died instantly

---

[86] See Appendix for a complete list of major naval ships deployed 25 miles outside of Girón Beach. The Navy was under strict orders from the President not to intervene in the conflict.

[87] Batallón de Jefatura – HQ Battalion

[88] Damn, I'm in a John Wayne movie....

When we got to the beach we passed by one of the newly built cinder block houses. The house had been strafed by 20 mm shells and there was one of our guys sitting on the floor that had taken a direct hit to the head. I now realize who this casualty was after reading Enrique's account.

Enrique Saavedra continued on to the beach and happened to find the group from the Headquarters Battalion. José San Román, the Brigade commander, was on the radio talking to the navy flotilla clearly visible from the beach. Enrique heard San Román imploring them to act now or the Brigade would be massacred. The response he received was that the Navy had orders to NOT participate in any support or rescue mission. San Román then gave the order to all troops in Girón Beach to go through the swamp and link up with Guerrilla forces in the Escambray mountains.

We linked up to Brigade HQ on the beach later that afternoon and got those same orders to go into the swamp and try to make it to the Escambray mountains to link up with the guerrillas fighting there. There was no sign of the American Navy or Naval Aviation anywhere. El Cadete[89] gave us our orders, into the brush we went.

Air Operations – Wednesday April 19

THE FOUR AIRMEN KILLED

Leo Baker   Wade Gray   Riley Shamburger   T.W. "Pete" Ray

Image 43: *Four Members of the Alabama Air National Guard killed flying volunteer missions over Girón*

---

[89] El Cadete – Henry Rodriguez - our squad leader

Two flights piloted by American Advisors flew from Nicaragua at 02:30 and 03:00. These brave men, all officers from the Alabama Air National Guard knew that they had been ordered not to fly during the invasion; they volunteered their lives to help their Cuban counterparts that had been betrayed by the liberal bureaucracy in Washington.

Both planes were shot down by T-33's while conducting attacks on enemy ground positions. Shamburger and Ray's plane splashed into the sea a few miles from Girón.

Gray and Baker were shot down near Central Australia. It is believed that both pilots were alive after crash landing their plane and were murdered by Castro militiamen. In a bizarre twist, the cuban military kept the body of Lieutenant Pete Ray in a freezer for 18 years, His body was released to his daughter who mounted a successful campaign in Congress to have her father's remains returned to the US.

The Celia

Image 44: Alejandro del Valle – Brigade's 1st Battalion (Airborne) Commander

One last tragic story concerning events at Playa Girón. Twenty two Brigade members, including our Battalion Commander, Alejandro del Valle and a member of my squad, Ernesto Hernández Cosío found a small abandoned fishing boat called "Celia" in Playa Girón on Wednesday. They decided to take a chance and try to sail the boat towards the American fleet visible in the distance. They were not picked up and drifted along the Gulf Stream.

There was no water or food onboard the Celia when they boarded her. They drifted for sixteen days pushed by the Gulf Stream current in the western Caribbean and the Gulf of Mexico; they were picked up by a commercial freighter South of New Orleans near the mouth of the Mississippi River.

Terrible stories are told of the horrors they endured during the voyage. There were twelve survivors left of the original group when they were picked up by the freighter; Alejandro del Valle and Ernesto Hernández Cosío (a member of our squad) did not make it.

La Ciénaga

Image 45. Ciénaga de Zapata - Matanzas, Cuba

When resistance on the Beach collapsed on Wednesday evening, April 19th, Castro ordered the formation of concentric troop rings starting at the main roads leading from Central Australia and Central Covadonga to Playa Larga and Playa Girón respectively. They had used this tactic successfully to eliminate the resistance fighters in El Escambray. In addition he deployed military helicopters to search for the Brigade troops that had dispersed into the swamps. Their orders were to shoot first and capture any of the Brigade members that surrendered to be transported to La Habana.

My brother Armando and I spent twelve days in the swamp until we stumbled into a Medical Brigade encampment near Central Covadonga. During that period of time we did not eat any solid food with the exception of a majá snake we captured while resting under a bush. We skinned the snake, removed the guts and passed a couple of lit matches under it to get rid of the wild flavor. We did not dare to build a fire due to the constant flight of helicopters in our vicinity. The snake was delicious!!!!

Image 46: Cuban majá snake – it is in the tree boa family

We moved at night and had to cross five of the troop rings. The troops were at a distance where they could see one another. In many of these crossings we were spotted and fired on, we were again lucky we were not hit. We survived on water trapped on holes in the calcareous rocks which were everywhere and by eating the snake.

Finally on the first of May we were so weak from malnutrition that we blacked out when we stood up. We stumbled unawares into the camp of a Cuban militia battalion's medical unit. Again our Guardian Angel was with us, the commanding officer, a doctor, was very kind to us and gave each one of us a can of condensed milk. To this day I can drink condensed milk straight out of a can and it tastes like the most delicious food ever. My brother started to try to convince the militia interrogators that we were peasants. I told my brother that the gig was up and that we would be shot for sure.

They put us on a bus that afternoon along with some troops and sent us to El Palacio de los Deportes in the Alturas del Vedado section of La Habana; this was a huge stadium built during the Batista era, where we were to be exhibited like animals in the zoo to the fawning international press corps.

The Bus stopped in the central square or park of every major town in the route. Thousands of people would descend on the bus and punch the sides yelling Paredón, Paredón!!![90] It was very hard for me to accept that I had risked my life to bring freedom to this country; if the guards in the bus would not have followed their orders, we would have been lined up against a wall and shot on the spot many times.

I told my brother during the long trip to get ready for the worst. I was convinced that true to their past performance, we would be sent to the firing squad.

This was our triumphal parade to La Habana that we were promised by our American advisors in Nicaragua.

---

[90] Paredon – put them in front of the firing wall

La Rastra[91]

Image 47: *Brigade Prisoners Awaiting Transport to La Habana*

I was very lucky to be captured late and avoided some of the horrific events some of my fellow Brigade members endured immediately after being taken prisoners by the Castro forces. For many years the Bay of Pigs Veterans Association has filed unsuccessful lawsuits with International Tribunals[92] denouncing one incident that occurred that involved Comandante Osmani Cienfuegos of the Ejército Rebelde and the transport of Brigade prisoners from Playa Girón to La Habana.

---

[91] La Rastra – the trailer portion of an eighteen wheeler truck.
[92] Lawsuits filed by members of the Asociación de Veteranos de Bahía de Cochinos: 2006 Tribunal Español – Querella Sobre Derechos Humanos and in 2012 Appeal to European Court of Human Rights in Strasbourg, Germany.

Facts As Outlined in Human Rights Abuse Lawsuits

Plaintiffs: Comite de Ayuda a la Disidencia – On behalf of surviving members of Brigade 2506 Represented by Juan R López de la Cruz, Juan J González, and the brothers Francisco and Emilio Valdés Calderón

Defendants: Fidel Castro, Head of Cuban State, Commander in Chief of Cuban Armed Forces, First Secretary of Cuban Communist Party, and Comandante Osmani Cienfuegos – Ejército Rebelde and Director of Public Works

Charges:

During the period of April 20th to April 22nd 1961 the plaintiffs along with other surviving members of Brigade 2506 were captured and imprisoned in small houses alongside Playa Girón Cuba after the Brigade was defeated by approximately 62,000 soldiers of the Cuban armed forces.

These initial prisoners were not given any water or food by the Rebel Army soldiers guarding them during this period. They were insulted, spat upon and prodded with bayonets. They were repeatedly told that they were "worms" and that they would be executed soon

On the 22nd of April, these prisoners who numbered one hundred and forty men, including those wounded in combat, were lined up in front of a refrigerated tractor trailer rig. Comandante Osmani Cienfuegos under direct orders from Fidel Castro who was personally commanding all Cuban forces in the Girón area, gave the order to load all prisoners into this airtight trailer.

When told by one of the prisoners that they would all die from asphyxia his reply was: "It does not matter, we are going to execute all of you anyway. This way we will save the ammunition"

The interior of the trailer was paneled with wood, making it impossible for air to seep in from the outside. The doors were sealed and due to the high temperature outside the rig, exhaled breath began to condense on the roof and sweat began to "rain" on the prisoners inside.

Soon because of the large number of prisoners closely packed inside the rig, horrible scenes began to play out as men screamed that they were suffocating and were about to die.

Some prisoners on the back and center areas of the trailer were able to make a couple of small holes using their belt buckles; these were not sufficient to ventilate the trailer so helping hands would pass the bodies of those dying from asphyxia up so that they could get a breath of air.

A Brigade member shouted to his fellow troopers to try to remain calm as this would prolong the quantity of breathable air in the trailer.

The rig made several stops on the way to La Habana. Shouts and pleas by the prisoners inside were answered with threats:

"We don't care if you all suffocate; shut up or we are going to machine gun you all"

During the long trip an incident occurred that was burned into all their minds, Brigade Member José Millan sat up and told Emilio Valdes sitting next to him. "I am about to die, I am seeing Jesus in front of me, please tell my wife and children in Miami what happened. Jesus told me that many of you would be saved"

Nine hours later the rig pulled up in front of the Palacios de Los Deportes (a sports stadium in La Habana). The doors were open and as the prisoners stumbled out they could clearly see the bodies of their comrades lying on the floor of the truck. Nine men died during this trip.

The direct responsibility for these atrocities lie on the shoulders of Comandante Osmani Cienfuegos who gave the direct order to load these prisoners on the sealed trailer.

I am also reprinting here a piece by Billy Muir, who is a first cousin of my wife Margarita and who was involved in what can at best be described as first degree mass murder

La Rastra Murders - A Witness' Story

By William D Muir

It was April 22nd, 1961. We woke up in Girón, a small town at the tip of the Bay of Pigs. We were captured the night before by Castro's militia. After two and a half days of intense fighting and two and a half days trying to escape through the Zapata swamps, we were exhausted. Our last meal was on Sunday, April 16th, aboard the Houston. Since then, all we had to sustain us was water, what we carried in our canteens and what we scooped from the rain puddles.

That was it.

A group of 'milicianos' (Castro's militia) escorted us down to the beach, to Comandante Osmany Cienfuegos. He sat stoically at a table. One by one we were interrogated:

"What's your name?",

"Where do you live?",

"Who were your parents?",

"What is your occupation?".

Depending on the answers, insults rained down. I used Guillermo Muir Celorio instead of William Dennis Muir Celorio, to avoid being branded as English, or even worse, an American.

After the interrogation ended, we were loaded into a trailer as if we were cargo. The 18-wheeler, made entirely of steel, was used to transport tobacco. The only access was one side door and the double back doors. The owner of the truck line, a Brigade member, told Comandate Cienfuegos that people would die if the doors were to be closed.

We laid the more badly wounded toward the front. When literally no one else was able to fit, the doors were closed.

Darkness…

In the darkness, you could not see your hand in front of you. It was extremely hot, over 100 degrees. We could not breathe. All the oxygen was gone. It was so loud you could not hear the person next to you.

Then the trip began; we did not know where we were going. We assumed we would be killed upon arrival, wherever that was. The 114-mile trip from Girón to Havana began around noon. It should have taken around three hours, but it took over eight.

At the joints of the steel plates, we rubbed our belt buckles trying to allow any air to flow. After taking numerous turns, finally a small amount of air greeted us. We took turns breathing. Several people who were almost passed out were given priority. We did not know who they were, all we knew was that they needed oxygen.

Desperation…

Desperate times call for desperate measures. We were convinced that we were going to die anyways, either from suffocation during the trip or being killed on arrival. So we came up with a plan. We would rock from side to side and cause the whole thing to tumble over. Some would be killed in the crash, some would survive the crash; some would be killed by the milicianos, but some would be able to escape. Over all the noise, we were able to start swaying the trailer.

All of a sudden, the truck stopped, and we heard loud noises outside. I cannot confirm, but I suspect, the milicianos shot their machine guns. No one was hurt, but maybe, just maybe, the machine gun fire opened holes that would allow air to come in.

Arrival…

Finally, when the truck stopped and the back doors opened, a bunch of milicianos barked at us to get off. When my turn came to disembark, I stumbled to the floor and fell on my hands. When my hands hit the floor, they were covered in a disgusting combination of sweat and urine. As I was trying to get up, I felt a body on the ground. The body was cold. He was dead. He was right next to me the entire time and I had never even felt him.

We had arrived at El Palacio de los Deportes, a dome-type basketball arena. It turned out that they were not going to kill us after all. However, 9 men lay dead, asphyxiated during the eight hour trip.

Hypocrisy…

Now sitting in the stands, as spectators of a sporting event, we were given water. Fidel Castro appeared and, with incredible hypocrisy, blamed the truck driver for the incident.

Honor…

Let's honor those that gave their lives in these horrible circumstances:

Alfredo José Cervantes Lago

José Ignacio Macía del Monte

José Santos Millán Velasco,

Hermillo Benjamín Quitana Pereda,

Santos Ramos Álvarez

Pedro Rojas Mir

Moisés Santana González

René Silva Soublete

José Daniel Vilarello Tabares.

Signed: William D Muir – witness

PRISON

El Palacio de los Deportes

Image 48: Palacio de los Deportes – La Habana

We arrived at the Palacio de los Deportes, a huge sports stadium built during the Batista regime, on May 2nd. My brother and I were among the last to be captured and we were spared the spectacle of Fidel grandstanding for the press and the public interrogations of some selected Brigade officers.

Tomas Cruz was a member of the Paratrooper Battalion and commanded Company A. He was of Afro-Cuban descent. He was asked by Fidel:

Don't you know that your yankee friends do not allow people of your race to go to a public beach?

Cruz's answer is a classic

"Comandante, I did not come here to go to the beach."

Erneido Oliva was second in command of the Brigade. He too was from Afro-Cuban descent. He did not betray the United States while being interrogated.

After his release from prison, Oliva and Cruz volunteered to join the United States Army. Oliva served in the 82nd Airborne and was deployed to the Dominican Republic. He left the regular army and joined the District of Columbia's National Guard where he went on to have a distinguished military career and advanced in rank to Major General.

Image 49: *President Reagan congratulates Erneido Oliva on his appointment to Major in the DC National Guard. He later advanced in rank to Major General in the Guard.*

When the press left town, we were bused to a naval hospital that was still under construction and which became our prison home for a couple of months.

El Hospital Naval

Image 50: *Hospital Naval 1962 – Habana del Este Cuba*

Shortly after my brother and I arrived at the Palacio de los Deportes we boarded another set of buses and were driven to the Hospital Naval in La Habana del Este[93] This facility, built during the Batista presidency, was still under construction. We were housed here because it was a vacant building, so it was easy to establish security and cut off access to family, friends or the press.

I remember one day when Fidel Castro came to visit the prisoners. He was very complimentary of the Brigade's fighting spirit and promised the people in my room that if they would denounce the Yanqui imperialists and join the Fuerzas Armadas Revolucionarias, all would be forgiven.

There were no takers.

---

[93] El Hospital Naval – the Navy Hospital – construction on the current building started in 1956 by the Batista Government, it was planned to be a modern hospital for members of the Cuban Navy. All work stopped in 1959 when Castro came to power. Construction resumed after we transferred to other prisons and the hospital was used to treat casualties from the Cuban government's many incursions in foreign countries.

At that time Castro was trying to exchange us for Tractors, when these negotiations stalled, we were back on the buses again, this time our destination was the Castillo del Príncipe.

El Castillo del Príncipe[94]

In June the entire brigade was transferred to one of Castro's most notorious detention facilities for political prisoners. The Castillo del Príncipe was a fortress constructed in 1767 as part of the fortifications the Spanish government erected to defend La Habana from pirates and the English navy. It was used by the Castro government at that time as a penal institution for common criminals and political dissidents.

Image 51: *Castillo del Príncipe – Loma de Aróstegui, La Habana*

---

[94] El Castillo del Príncipe – The Castle of the Prince

Prison Life

The Brigade prisoners were assigned to locations inside the prison alphabetically based on their last name. Since our last name began with a B we were assigned to an area called the Vivac that had four large rectangular prisoner holding cells. We were with the B's in Galera 2, a large room with one sink, one toilet and 60 metal frames with canvas stretched across forming a lower and upper bunk. In addition to the sink there was a water faucet on high that would serve as a crude shower.

We each were issued one pair of blue denim pants and a yellow t-shirt. Everyone had to wear these and you had only one pair. There were 120 people living in our room. There were four galeras[95] in our area which had a capacity for approximately 450 people. We were shut in, not allowed to go outside and incommunicado, no contact with the outside world.

Our guards were chosen from units that fought against us in Girón, so there was no love lost between us. They were there 24x7. They were forbidden to speak to us so we had no idea of what was going on outside. At approximately 7 pm lights would blink and there was no further talking or noises allowed. The lights would stay on all night.

Failure to follow orders would result in a quick visit by the armed guards and the culprit taken outside and disciplined. The guards had orders not to talk to us so we had no contact with the outside world.

These were dark nights indeed, even though the electric lights were on full blast, inside our minds it was very, very dark….

We were forbidden to look out the barred windows (our galera did not have windows that looked outside so this was not a problem for us in Galera 2), In the Sanatorio[96] failure to stop looking out-

---

[95] Galeras – long rectangular rooms with high stone walls, designed to hold prisoners.
[96] Sanatorio – the castle's area for medical treatment had been converted into a prison cell

side would result in the guards firing at the culprit. This actually happened several times in this cell block, facing the University of La Habana where coeds would stand to get a look at us.

Food came in a large aluminum container and we each had a tin plate, spoon and cup. We each received one ladle full of whatever food staple the country had a surplus (so bad that people on ration cards would not eat it). A typical example is that during one stretch of time (about a month) we ate boiled pumpkin. Another favorite of the cooks were these small Chinese beans we called "patria o muerte"[97].

We only got one ladle full, you ate your food quickly so you could go to the end of the line and get seconds – this was known as re-enganche (hook on again) – It would stop as soon as the guard recognized that you had been fed before.

On occasion the cooks would play cruel tricks on us. Their favorite was to kill a rat and stick it in the aluminum food container… That was the only real meat available….

The Tractors for Prisoners Committee

In May of 1961 President Kennedy had received several hints from Fidel Castro to consider trading the Bay of Pigs prisoners for agricultural tractors. The basis for this offer by Castro was an episode in Spanish History during Napoleon's occupation of Spain where the rebel Spanish groups had asked Napoleon to consider trading captured French troops for pigs. This is revealing because it gives us a glimpse into Fidel Castro's convoluted mind. The Brigade was consistently referred to in Castro's propaganda machine (the Cuban press) as "gusanos" (worms) or lumpen (lowest strata of society); by making this offer Castro would again debase his opposition while gaining tangible assets he could showcase as having helped the poor peasants.

---

[97] Patria o muerte – fatherland or death – a favorite crowd chant during Fidel's all night harangues. Attendance was mandatory.

John and Bobby Kennedy jumped on this offer and asked former first lady Eleanor Roosevelt, UAW President Walter Reuthers, Milton Eisenhower, brother of the ex-president and President of John Hopkins University and former Eisenhower Budget Director Joseph Dodge to form a committee to secure the funding, define the terms and arrange for the exchange of the prisoners. Mrs. Roosevelt was given the Chairmanship of the Committee.

The impact of these negotiations on our prison life was that the Castro government allowed for families to visit us and bring food during the visits. All of my immediate family with the exception of my grandmother was already in the States, so my brother and I had to be happy with food donations from our fellow inmates.

I have been asked many times over the years this question: How did the guards treat you?

The truthful response is this – when the negotiations for our release were "on" – the quality of the food increased (it was edible), visitors were allowed and there was less physical abuse – when they were "off" – we were completely isolated, no communication with the outside, the guards or other inmates. Rules were strictly enforced and failure to comply brought on a swift response.

One episode illustrates how seriously they enforced this. There was an area where some of the prisoners were kept, it was called "el sanatorio" because it had been used previously as a place to hold sick inmates. There was a rule that you could not look out the windows, but unfortunately for us there were some nurses from a hospital across from the castle that knew we were there and started waving at these windows. One morning the militiaman on guard just opened fire on the prisoners waving back and several brigade members were hit. No one looked out the windows after that.

The Great Escape

In 1961 Johnny López de la Cruz and José Dearin González-Morejón in the Vivac area noticed that one of the brigade prisoners was making rope out of discarded jute sacs used by the guards to bring bread to the prisoners. As the first negotiations for the prisoner's exchange had been terminated they thought it was possible to use this rope to escape from the prison area we were in. They darkened their yellow t-shirts and began to closely watch the guard's movements across the moat from the Vivac. We had been allowed to use an enclosed patio to get some fresh air once a week since the negotiations started for the tractors for prisoners exchange. One stormy night they noticed the guard was not at his post and they decided to go for it. Johnny and José jumped the wall and climbed down the rope into the moat that separated the prison from the outer wall. They were able to climb up the outer wall and sneak into the street.

Image 52: *Entrance to Castillo del Príncipe*

They wandered the streets of La Habana and wound up in Marianao after trying to find someone who would help them. Both were recaptured and brought back and placed in solitaire.

All visiting and patio privileges for all prisoners were suspended after this episode. Within a few days we were moved within the prison and housed in the "Leoneras".[98]

Johnny volunteered for the United States Army after his release, served in Europe and Vietnam, and rose to the rank of Colonel. He retired from the military and is the President of the Brigade 2506 Veterans Association as of the writing of this book.

The Trial

Image 53: *Brigade Trial – Castillo del Príncipe – July 1962*

On September 8, of 1961 in a secret trial, 14 Brigade members were convicted of treason and other high crimes. Five were executed by firing squad and the rest sentenced to 30 years' hard labor. Following typical communist procedure the fourteen mem-

---

[98] Leoneras – literally means lion dens, dungeon level cells facing the moats directly

bers were chosen arbitrarily and the sentences were totally unrelated to their prior offenses. No one from the Brigade's military or political leadership was indicted in this farcical trial.

El Juicio de la Brigada – William D Muir

Days before the trial

The Brigade's legal minds came up with a strategy: we would not offer any testimony. No matter what the consequences, we would not say a word. This would mean that we did not recognize the judge's authority.

Around 4 in the evening, the day before the trail was to start, Caron, an incredibly good musician, began chanting the refrain "Tú ves, yo no lloro". Loosely translated "See, I don't cry". The four cell blocks: Vivac, Sanatorio, Galera 15-19 and Enfermería join in, louder and louder. And it continued all night long, not a soul got a drop of sleep that night.

Coming down

All the cell blocks were on the top floor of "El Castillo del Príncipe". The 1,300 surviving men were brought down to the center court through two small stairways. They were pushed by armed militia men with bayonets. Shouting and insults guided us to the pews, there was a lot of pushing and Torres Mena (a Brigade member) was stabbed with a bayonet. He punched the militia man back, his weapon fell and a big disturbance started. More and more people were joining in the mêlée.

Pomponio, as we called the prison commander, ran to the front of the pews, where San Román, Brigade Commander, Oliva second in command and Artime civil leader were sitting and screamed, "You have to stop this".

Oliva walked to the microphone on the stage, stood at attention and commanded "Brigada Atención". The entire Brigade snapped to attention, reflecting the well trained military unit we were. He then began "Al combate corred Bayameses…." The words of the Cuban national anthem. We sang as loud as we possibly could, even some of the militia men joined in the singing. At the end Oliva ordered us to sit.

3 days on trial

First the prosecution presented all the "crimes" we had committed during the war. Then the defense repeated the list of crimes and agreed with the prosecution. The fix was obvious. For 3 days we heard the same, over and over. At every moment they would try for any one of us to come up and testify. Suddenly an arm went up, the prosecutor could not hide his happiness. What do you want to say, come to the microphone, he said. "I just want to go to the bathroom", said the Brigade member.

Finally the sentence was read, 30 years hard labor for each member of the Brigade.

I thought my future consisted of thirty years cutting sugar cane, in Cuba there was no parole for political prisoners. But life goes on, and always surprises us.

In the Lion's Den

Image 54: *Entrance to the "Leoneras"*

The period from July to December 1962 was marked by a series of ups and downs. Life was pretty grim in the Leoneras but we were a pretty resourceful group.

The Charanga Band

We had formed a band in our Galera in which my brother played. He was one of the founders since he could play the guitar very well. They called themselves "La Charanga de Caron" [99] named after the brigade member that started it. They used "prison - made" instruments, drums made out of empty tin cracker containers, "horns" were made from empty bottles with cellophane membranes, there were two guitars that family members had brought to their relatives during the family visits, etc. Many prisoners sang in this band and also in a chorale that had been formed. After we were released the Charanga band was invited to play in the Ed Sullivan show and gave a performance in Ed's show on January 13 of 1963.

The Missile Crisis

Although we were in total isolation during October and November of 1962 we knew that something was happening of major importance due to the increase in the number of guards and the disappearance of militia guards who were replaced by regular FAR soldiers who were heavily armed.

The final tip off for our Galera, came one day in October when a detachment of regular troops started to drill holes into the stone walls high near the ceiling where we could not reach. We asked them what it was that they were doing. The response:

"Si vienen los yankees ustedes son los primeros que se mueren."[100]

---

[99] Caron's Charanga Band. A charanga band is an amateur group of musicians playing on homemade instruments

[100] If the Yankees come you will be the first to die

We realized that they were stuffing the holes with explosives.

During this time some of the prisoners were relocated to the former Presidio Modelo in the Cuban island Isla de Pinos. [101] Included in this group were many of the military and political leaders of the Brigade. My brother and I and most of the remaining surviving prisoners, remained in the Castillo del Príncipe

Christmas 1962

After the standoff between the United States and the Soviet Union over the introduction of Medium Range Ballistic Missiles into Cuban territory resulting in the removal of missiles in Cuba and Turkey and the signing of a secret protocol assuring the Soviets that the US would not invade Cuba or allow Cuban exile groups to continue attacks on Cuban territory[102].

Castro renewed his offer to exchange the Brigade prisoners for a set sum. Prisoners were divided into 3 groups and different amounts were assigned based on Castro's evaluation of the family's ability to pay. The one with wealthier families had to pay a price of $100,000 to be ransomed. The ones with middle class families $ 50,000. The ones from poor families had a price tag of $ 25,000. My brother and I had a price tag of $ 50K. My parents did not have anywhere near that kind of money.

James Donovan, a lawyer that took part in the Nuremberg trials and subsequently acquired extensive experience negotiating with the Soviet Union (he was instrumental in the release of downed

---

[101] Isla de Pinos – large island located south of the main island of Cuba – Castro renamed it Isla de la Juventud. It housed the largest prison in Cuba, Presidio Modelo, virtually escape proof

[102] Contrary to media reporting the Missile Crisis resulted in a US defeat since the Soviet Union still had a base in Cuba and used it to refuel nuclear subs and aircraft that loitered outside the US coast. The Soviet primary activities in Cuba were to use it as a spying post, a training and staging base for military incursions and a propaganda base to destabilize pro-US governments in Latin America and elsewhere – [see introduction]

U2 pilot Francis Power as part of the settlement regarding the release of captured Soviet spy Col. Rudolf Abel) was asked to assume control of the negotiations. He accepted the assignment and flew to Cuba to establish a personal rapport with Fidel Castro. He returned to the US with a firm commitment from the Cuban government to release the prisoners if the ransom amount of $ 53 million dollars was paid.

Donovan met with the president of Pfizer Corporation, an important pharmaceutical manufacturer to brainstorm how the ransom could be paid. A deal was struck with Bobby Kennedy that would allow Pfizer and other Pharmaceutical and Food Corporations to donate merchandise valued at the demanded ransom amount and then deduct that amount from their corporate tax bills. The deal was completed and the release date set for Christmas 1962.

Flying Home

On December 25 1962 we boarded buses that took us to the main DAAFAR[103] air base at San Antonio de los Baños. We boarded a stripped down Pan American Airways cargo DC6 and enjoyed the best plane ride of our lives in the cargo hold. We landed at Homestead Air Force Base, south of Miami. After a delicious meal complete with ice cream and glasses of milk, we were taken to a number of waiting buses and driven to Dinner Key Auditorium where we were reunited with our family members.

No CIA official was present, no debriefing was done upon our return. To this day, (59 years later), I have not spoken to anyone from the agency about my two years of "service".

My love for the United States, (I became a citizen in 1967), is very strong. My respect for the individuals that planned the Bay of Pigs operation and the politicians that doomed it to failure is not very high.

---

[103] DAAFAR – Cuban Revolutionary Anti Aircraft Defenses and Air Forces

Image 55: *The Author is reunited with his baby brother Peter at Dinner Key Auditorium Dec 25 1962*

Image 56: *President John F Kennedy receives Brigade Flag from Erneido Oliva*

During the act at the Orange Bowl in January 1962, President Kennedy accepted the Brigade's Flag and promised to return it in a free Cuba. After many years of waiting for this promise to be kept, the Kennedy family eventually returned the flag to the Brigade's Veteran Association.

Happy Ending - Life in the States

Image 57: *Margarita and I at our wedding – St Charles Catholic Church, Arlington VA*

On the fourth of July 1963 I met the love of my life in Fairfax Lake Virginia. We were married a year and a half later, and have been happily married for over 56 years. We have four wonderful children and nine grandchildren. We are very proud of all of them.

When I returned to the States I resumed my University studies. I could not continue my Civil Engineering degree since there were no evening classes offered, and I had to work. I was able to graduate from college (American University and Georgia State University), received a Masters degree in finance from Georgia State, and became a CPA in the State of Georgia. I am very proud that I worked my way through college (seven years to get my undergraduate degree) and received no financial aid. I worked as a consultant for a major CPA firm, and for Kurt Salmon Associates, a consulting firm from which I retired. I started my own consulting business and had the privilege of doing major projects for companies like IBM, Southern Company and Levi Strauss. My last full time job was with EMS Technologies (now Honeywell) from which I retired for the second time in 2006.

Life has been very good to me and I live in the beautiful town of Peachtree Corners in the state of Georgia.

Special Friends

Life is full of deeply ironic twists. When I was transferred in 1960 by BP Oil to work in their new North American Headquarters in Atlanta, I met two families that became lifelong friends.

I met Galo Cimadevilla at a men's catholic retreat in the Trappist Monastery of the Holy Spirit in Conyers, Georgia. We were seated at the same table and it was not long until we had developed a strong friendship. Galo was very outgoing and he had that wonderful Cuban mix of seriousness and laughter. They had three wonderful children and we had four, so Margarita, my wife and Marta, his wife, had lots of great stories to share.

I found out that Galo and I shared an amazing episode in our pasts. Galo's cousin was in the Ejército Rebelde and had fought against Batista. His cousin was a personal friend of Fidel Castro and talked Galo into joining the militia forces. On April 17, his cousin called him on the phone and told him to grab his weapons and drive to the Central Covadonga where Fidel had established his headquarters. You will recall that my unit's objective was to cut the road linking Playa Girón to the Central Covadonga. We had actually been facing each other on the same battlefield during those fateful April days!

On August 26, 2019 I walked into his house moments after he had passed away. I had the distinct honor of being asked by his wife and children to speak at his funeral. May you be at peace my Galito, be at peace my friend.

The second family is the Berenguer family. We met Cesar and Carmen shortly after moving to Georgia. There was a huge ice storm in January of 1973, power went out throughout the city and was not restored for a week. Luckily the Berenguers lived in a home with a fireplace and we found ourselves camping in their living room. Our friendship has continued until the present day, I am known to the Berenguers as Rolo, a character I created to be the hero of many bedtime stories I told their kids.

During the Invasion of Playa Girón, Cesar was in the militias (it was mandatory if you wanted to work) and spent much of the month of April laying communication lines to hook up the Ejército Rebelde outposts to their field headquarters in Playa Girón.

What are the odds that two of my best friends of over 50 years would have been involved in this historical event, but fought for the opposing side? This life lesson has helped me to be a better person and provided much needed perspective in dealing with others in my professional and personal life. It also taught me the value of humility and forgiveness.

There is a third group of special friends. They are the veterans of the Brigade. Many have read this manuscript and contributed to its content and veracity. In Margarita's family, Billy Muir and Enrique Saavedra contributed their stories and I have given them credit as I cited them. My very good friends Rafael Montalvo, Pepe Irastorza and Henry Rodríguez fact checked the first drafts. My brother Armando sent me emails with reminders of incidents that I did not mention. Retired Col Juan (Johnny) López de la Cruz contributed material on his escape from prison and the subsequent legal actions taken by the Brigade to try to convict Osmany Cienfuegos and Fidel Castro for the atrocities committed against Brigade members after their capture.

I often think of the members of the Brigade that didn't make it, many were good friends and many more strangers. They gave their life to free that beautiful island of my youth.

In 1960 I volunteered to fight for the island and country of my birth; today I would not hesitate to volunteer again to fight to defend the country that adopted me and my wife. The United States of America. One of my sons was in the Marines, and two of my grandchildren currently serve in the armed forces of the United States (USMC and US Navy). I am especially proud of them for their service to our country.

I keep telling myself that there will be a day of reckoning, when the truth will be told, when the culprits will be unmasked, when the lies will be refuted. That day is still in the future. Probably, it will not come in my lifetime…

APPENDICES

Appendix 1

Table 2. Brief Timeline of Cuban History (1492 to 1958)

A. Spanish Colonial Period – 1492 to 1898

B. US Intervention – 1898 to 1902

C. First Cuban Republic – 1902 to 1958

	Spanish Colonial Period	
27 October 1492	Columbus explores north coast of Cuba	Writes in his diary: This is the most beautiful land that human eyes have seen
1510 to 1513	First Settlements	Baracoa - Bayamo - Trinidad - Sancti Spiritus - La Habana - Santiago de Cuba
1566 to 1790	La Habana is Central Caribbean Port to Spanish West Indies Fleet	Cuba becomes central hub for Spanish trade with Central and South America
Sixteenth Century	Expansion of Sugar and Tobacco Plantations	Period sees introduction of slavery and constant attacks by pirates, corsairs and bucaneers
1728	Universidad de La Habana is founded by the Dominican Preaching Order	Many of Cuba's leaders in its fight for independence attended this excellent University. The Univeridad de la Habana has always been free to all Cuban citizens.
1762 - 1763	Capture of the City of La Habana by the British	During the Seven Year War British Forces attacked and captured the city of La Habana. A fleet of 53 ships carrying nearly 20000 men attacked June 6 1762. Spain recovered Cuba in 1763 when it traded it for Florida which had been a Spanish colony.
1812 and 1844	Slave Insurrection of 1812 and Conspiracion de la Escalera in 1844	In 1812 Jose Antonio Aponte a free black man of Yoruba origin was tried and executed along with 50 men. La Conspiracion de la Escalera resulted from false rumors that black and mulatto free cubans were going to stage a revolt - this was followed by savage repression by the Spanish authorities
1851	Invasion by Gen Narciso Lopez and Southern US Annexation Movement	In the 1850's many southern states saw an opportunity to increase their political power by annexing Cuba. This movement was funded by private individuals. Gen Narciso Lopez from Venezuela was chosen to lead a group of southern volunteers. They were defeated and executed.
1853	Conspiracion Soles y Rayos de Bolivar	Inspired by Simon Bolivar's dream of a unified confederation of Central and South American Nations. Conspirators met in masonic lodges. Six hundred people arrested in La Habana, Camaguey and Trinidad.
1853 to 1868	Increased Nationalistic Conscience	Educators like Father Felix Varela teaching in the Seminario de San Carlos, Rafael Maria de Mendive in the Escuela Superior Municipal de Varones and Jose de la Luz y Caballero founder of Colegio El Salvador created national conscience in their students, specially Jose Marti
1868 to 1878	First War of Indepence also known as The Ten Years War	Full scale war against spanish troops. Carlos Manuel de Cespedes freed his slaves and proclaimed Cuba independent. Casualties: Cubanos: 50,000 (est) Spanish:81,248
1879 to 1880	La Guerra Chiquita (The Tiny War)	Cuban General Calixto Garcia repudiates the Zanjon Peace Treaty that ended the Ten Years war and wages war against the Spanish for two years. War ended due to divisions among Cuban factions and exiled cubans in US
1895 to 1898	War of Independence	Jose Marti galvanizes Cuban exiles in Tampa, New York, Fernandina Beach, Santo Domingo D.R. Venezuela, Guatemala and Mexico. In 1895 he lands in Cuba with General Maximo Gomez to join rebel forces in Oriente Province. A fierce war where Spanish troops under Valeriano Weyler committed war crimes against civilian population ended in 1898 with the entry of the US into the conflict, the sinking of the spanish fleet in Santiago de Cuba and the American Intervention in Cuba. Casualties: Cuban Rebels: 8,617 Cuban Civilians: 200,000 to 400,000 Spanish: 62,000+ US: 5,000

US Intervention

Date	Event	Details
1 January 1899	Gen John Brooks assumes command of US occupation army in Cuba	Appoints cubans to political posts - creates police and rural guards staffed with Cubans - implements public works and public health projects - National University and Institute of Secondary Education open in La Habana - Supreme Court and Judicial System created and staffed with cubans
20 December 1899	Gen Leonard C Wood assumes command of US occupation Army in Cuba	Civilian Government expanded and staffed by Cubans - Health Department created - Dr Carlos Finlay appointed to lead fight to eradicate yellow fever - creation of elementary education system - National Library created and staffed - census taken - 1,572,577 persons and 417,933 voters identified
16 June 1900	First Municipal Elections	City Mayors, Treasurers and Municipal Judges for a term of one year
5 November 1900	First Constitutional Convention	Constitution modeled on US - US demanded 3 things - orderly free government - political relationship with US defined and Constitutional Assembly restricted to creating constitution - Cuban Constitution was ammended by US congress Platt Ammendment which gave US power to intervene in Cuban affairs if US interests were threatened - very unpopular with cubans and was never exercized
2 January 1902	Presidential Elections	Tomas Estrada Palma elected first president of Cuban Republic
20 May 1902	End of US Intervention and creation of Republica de Cuba	Gen Wood transfers power to President Estrada Palma - Cuban flag raised over Morro Castle and the Palace of the Governor General - all US troops withdrawn from Cuba by the end of this day except for three army companies training cuban artillery gunners

	First Cuban Republic	
1902 to 1906	Presidency of Tomas Estrada Palma	Cuba's first president. Negotiated Treaty with US outlining Cuban American relations. US recognized Cuba's sovereignty over Isle of Pines. US was given 99 year lease of Guantanamo Bay to build Naval Base. Estrada Palma was honest and critical of corruption. Ran for re-election under conservative party. Election outcome was challenged and violence erupted. US sent in the Marines and an Administrator - Charles Magoo. US intervention lasted until 1909
1925 - 1933	Presidency of Gerardo Machado	Cuba's fifth president, Gerardo Machado was Major General in the Cuban War of Independence, later he became a businessman. Campaigned on "water, roads and schools". Built Cuba's Carretera Central - modern road that linked all Cuban provinces. Expanded and modernized Universidad de La Habana. Built the Cuban Capitol and many Health clinics and hospitals. Second term was marred by Great Depression in US and economic unrest in the island. Increased opposition was met by repression and revolution started in 1933. Machado lost US support of newly elected President Franklin D Roosevelt. Spearheaded by ABC student movement, a revolt by the NCO's in the army led by Sargent Fulgencio Batista toppled Machado who fled to the US.
1933 to 1940	Depression and Political Instability	ABC movement calls for General Strike. US Ambassador Summer Wells negotiates with opposition groups and Carlos Manuel de Cespedes is appointed as interim President. 4th of September 1933 Sargent Fulgencio Batista with support from Students assumes power and becomes head of the Army with a rank of Coronel. A series of interim governments sees 4 presidents in 3 years. In 1940 Batista is elected President. He serves one term.
1944 to 1952	Partido Autentico	1944 Ramon Grau San Martin is elected President. Cuba's economy continues to improve and Cuba's is staunch ally of the US against axis powers. He is followed by Carlos Prio Socarras elected in 1948. Economy flourishes but there is corruption and unrest among University students, with many incidents of violence.

148

1952 to 1956	Dictadura de Batista - First term	Fulgencio Batista returns from exile in the US and executes a coup d'etat on March 10 1952 with the support of the Army's general staff. Batista's first term sees increased economic expansion and achieves support through the construction of many infrastructure and public work projects. Tunnel under Bay of La Habana, expressway linking La Habana and Matanzas, Major highway providing access to southern La Habana, Matanzas and Las Villas provinces, Hospitals, Stadiums, and educational institutions. Political situation deteriorates with increased opposition from student groups and other political parties. 26 of July 1953 Fidel Castro, his brother and group of university students attacks army outpost Cuartel Moncada, Castro survives, is tried and is exiled due to intervention of Archbishop of Santiago de Cuba
1956 to 1958	Dictadura de Batista - Second Term	Increased political opposition from University Students (FEU) opposition political groups and rural areas. Directorio Revolucionario (student group) attacks presidential palace. Most of the attackers are killed. Increased level of violence in La Habana and the interior, bombings in movies, reprisals by army unit SIM and police, Fidel Castro and group of rebels lands in Oriente province in expedition financed by money from Carlos Prio Socarras ex-president of Cuba and Antonio del Conde who bought and restored the Yacht Granma used to take them to Cuba.
December 31 1958	Batista Flees Cuba	Without any adance warning Batista leaves Cuba in a military transport taking with him $300 million and 14 people, including family.

Policy Failures – Cuba Project

Why did the Invasion Fail and Who is to Blame?
Countless analysis and spin documents and media pieces have been written to explain the failure of the Cuban Invasion. The answer to this question is very simple.

The Policy of Plausible Deniability
The United States defined a key National Security Goal – in our story: **"overthrow the Castro government"**

The CIA under Allan Dulles created a plan to do it. It was drafted with DOD input. It called for three amphibious landings with full air and naval support.

There was a change in Administrations – The Democrats replaced the Republicans and a new young president took over

President Kennedy adopted Eisenhower's plan but did not have the guts to explain to the public the plan goals and components – so he ordered the CIA and the Department of State to create "official lies" to hide from the public what was evident that the United States was trying to do. He also lied to some of the key members of his team.[104]

The President then changed key aspects of the original plan making it less likely to succeed because he did not want the world to find out about the deceptions (the world would find out anyway when the US tried to implement his faulty modified plan). These changes included relocating and reducing the number of landing areas, and cancelling planned air strikes after the invasion started.

---

[104] A disastrous example of this toxic policy of keeping key players in the dark was the Kennedy brother's decision not to brief Adlai Stevenson, a former Kennedy political opponent and US Ambassador to the United Nations, on the facts surrounding the initial covert air strikes. Stevenson, in what can best be described as having a major temper tantrum, demanded that Kennedy stop any further air strikes. Kennedy complied. This decision doomed any remaining chance of success for the operation.

The President did not provide the teams that were trying to implement these plans with the material and tools to achieve the goal (adequate planes, ships, logistic support, etc)

The President hoped that through a miracle of God or a highly improbable combination of events his plan would succeed

It failed!!!!

The administration acts surprised. They started looking around for scapegoats...... First order of business is firing key implementation leaders.... But never the ones that caused it to fail....

Foreign Policy Impacts

The failure of the United States to depose the communist dictatorship of Fidel Castro in Cuba during the period 1961 – 1962 had enormous consequences that greatly exceeded the loss of prestige the United States suffered for such a failure.

Consider the following **facts** that are directly related to activities of the Cuban government run by the Castro brothers during the last sixty years.

Table 3 - Consequences of the Failure to Depose Castro in 1961

Cuban missile crisis – October1962 – World on the brink of nuclear war – end result was a draw – USSR removed missiles it had deployed – US gave up missile bases in Turkey and signed a secret treaty with the USSR guaranteeing the US would not remove the Castro regime by force.

Cuba continues to be a staging base, logistic supplier or military proxy of the USSR, China and other Communist governments:

October 1962 – Cuban military intervention in the Sand War in Algeria

1964 to 1967 – Cuban military provides military training and assistance to FALN guerrillas in Venezuela

1964 to 1965 – Cuban military assistance and troops to Republic of the Congo rebels

1965 to 1991 – Cuban military assistance and troops to Marxist rebels in Portuguese Guinea and Cabo Verde

1972 – Cuban military assistance and Cuban pilots to People's Republic of Yemen in Yemenite war of 1972

1967 to 1973 – Cuba trains commando group, provides military assistance and support to insurgents in Dominican Republic

1972 to 1975 – Soviets provided military equipment (including tanks). Cuba provided troops to fight with Syria in the Yom Kippur War of 1973

1973 to 1990 – Cuba is the main provider of support, training, logistical aid and Political assistance to communist MIR and FPMR guerrillas in Chile

1974 to 1988 – Military intervention in Angolan war supporting Marxist FAPLA (People's Armed Forces for the Liberation of Angola) Cuba provided 25,000 troops and supporting military equipment (including tanks)

1977 to 1978 – Ogaden War – Somali invasion of Ethiopia - Cuba deployed 18,000 troops; the Soviets provided armored cars, artillery, T-62 tanks, and MiGs to assist the Provisional Military Government of Socialist Ethiopia

1978 to 1990 – Military assistance to Marxist FLNS – Sandinista Front for National Liberation. Leaders of this guerrilla army were trained in Cuba, Cuba and Soviet Union provided military assistance and military intelligence personnel to Sandinista government

1979 to 1983 - Military assistance and troops to the People's Revolutionary Government of the Republic of Grenada. The Soviet Union, North Korea and Cuba provided military equipment and troops to this communist government. There were 800 to 1000 Cuban troops in Grenada when the US intervened in 1983

1980 to 1992 – Military and political assistance to communist guerrillas in El Salvador – Coordination of unification of different Marxist groups into one military – political organization FMLN

1964 to 2016 – Military and political assistance to the FARC guerrillas in Colombia – These guerrillas waged an open war against the Colombian people killing over 240,000 people over a period of 50 years. They specialized in kidnappings of prominent political and international figures and narco-terrorism. Cuba actively trained FARC leadership and assisted with political and logistical support. In 2016 Cuba brokered a cease fire between the Colombian Government and the FARC guerrillas.

1987 to Current Date – Cuba intervention in Venezuela – intervention in Venezuela's political affairs – training of key revolutionary figures by Cuban intelligence - By 2010, former Major General Antonio Rivero stated that about 92,700 Cuban officials were operating in various offices of Venezuela's government. Lately Venezuela and their Cuban advisors have cooperated with Iran who has purchased crude oil from Venezuela and in exchange has obtained a base in the Americas to promote Iranian terrorism and disseminate anti-american propaganda

Cuba continues to consistently obstruct United States policies in the Organization of American States, where it is still an active member, and in the United Nations.

Cuba has actively supported the following Marxist/socialist governments in Latin America and the Caribbean during the last sixty years

Nicaragua – Daniel Ortega
Chile – Salvador Allende
Ecuador – Rafael Correa and Lenin Moreno
Grenada – Maurice Bishop
Bolivia – Evo Morales
El Salvador – Mauricio Funes and Salvador Sánchez Cerén
Venezuela – Hugo Chávez and Nicolás Maduro

Cuba actively supported communist revolutionary movements that were **unable** to successfully overthrow the government of these countries:

April 1959 – Castro support for Coup in Panama

June 1959 – Invasion of Dominican Republic

1980-1992 – Castro support for Marxist Tupac Amaru Revolutionary guerrilla in Peru

1966 -1967 – Insertion of Che Guevara and Cuban guerrillas in Bolivia to aid Bolivian communist party to spark a popular revolution – Guevara was captured and executed by the Bolivian army

1980 to 1984 – Training and indoctrination of guerrillas of Alfaro Vive, Carajo terrorist group in Ecuador

Cuba operated a secret SIGINT (signal intelligence) station in Cuba from 1962 to 2002 to provide intelligence on US military, industrial and commercial activity to the Soviet Union and China. Located in La Habana's suburb of Lourdes, the facility covered an area of 73 km2 (28 sq mi). At its peak during the Cold War over 1,500 KGB, GRU, Cuban DGI, and Eastern Bloc technicians, engineers and intelligence operatives staffed the facility.

Cuba has operated several spy rings in the United States – the most notorious Cuban spy apprehended in the United States is Ana Belen Montes – she was a senior analyst at the Defense Intelligence Agency. Arrested in September 2001, she pleaded guilty and was convicted in October 2002.

Sixty one years have passed between the writing of this book and the events of April 17, 1961. The United States is still dealing with the consequences of what I consider to be the most terrible mistakes conducted by any US Administration in conducting foreign policy:

> Planning operations to achieve significant national interest objectives using people that do not have the adequate skills needed or intimate familiarity with the enemies of the United States

> Lying to the American public, lying to key American officials that were kept in the dark about ongoing operations, lying to the forces tasked to achieve these results and finally lying to the international community to advance policy objectives

> Failure to follow through by removing support from projects tasked to achieve these objectives

> Trying to cover up errors by blaming the wrong people, the ones that were pointing out these errors

A careful analysis of the Cuban project, as it was known in the intelligence community, will reveal that John Kennedy's administration committed all these mistakes in such a way that they still remain a college course case study of what NOT to do in similar circumstances.

Unfortunately the Cuban people are still paying the price.

Naval Units Involved In Bay of Pigs Invasion

US Navy Ships Deployed to "Escort" Bay of Pigs Invasion Ships

Image 58: *CV9 – USS Essex 1960's and CV21 USS Boxer*

Image 59: *There were 6 Destroyers in the task force – shown: DDE-576 USS Murray*

US Navy Ships Assigned to Directly Support Invasion Forces

Image 60: *LSD – 25 USS San Marcos – Tank and Heavy Equipment Carrier*

Image 61: *CIA Command and Control Ship - Barbara J*

The BLAGAR command ship of the Brigade's Navy, during the Bay of Pigs Operation. Commanded by Captain Juan Cosculluela and Grayston Lynch, American Invasion commander.

Image 62: CIA – LSI Class Ship – Invasion Navy Flagship Blagar

Colonel Juan R López de la Cruz
Fight for Human Rights

Facts in this book have been reviewed and edited by retired US Army Colonel Juan R López de la Cruz, who is the current president of the Bay of Pigs Veterans Association and who appears as one of the protagonists in one of the chapters of the book.

Image 63: *Colonel Juan (Johnny) López de la Cruz*

Colonel Juan (Johnny) López de la Cruz was commissioned in the U.S. Marine Corps in 1963 after participating as a paratrooper in the 1961 Bay of Pigs Invasion and subsequent imprisonment for almost two years as a POW in Cuba. Later, he transferred to the U.S. Army where he served for 26 years in various infantry, transportation and logistics positions.

His assignments included duties as Platoon Leader in Fort Benning, Georgia; Company Commander in Kaiserslautern, Germany and Pleiku, Vietnam; Battalion Executive Officer, Mekong Delta, Vietnam; Logistics Advisor to the Armed Forces of El Salvador and Battalion Commander in the Republic of Panama. In Panama he also served as Deputy Commander of the U.S. Army Security Assistance Agency for Latin America. He retired from the Army in 1989 after serving as Brigade Commander at the Oakland Army Base, California.

Colonel López graduated from the University of Nebraska with a degree in Business and attended various Senior Military Service Schools. His decorations include the Legion of Merit, three (3) Bronze Star Medals, three (3) Defense Service Medals, four (4) Meritorious Service Medals, The Air Medal, three (3) Joint Service Commendation Medals and four (4) Army Commendation Medals.

After retiring from the military service, Colonel López de la Cruz and his wife María made their home in Miami, Florida, where he founded a company that marketed Security and Defense products in the United States and Latin America. In 2018 he was elected President of the Bay of Pigs Veterans Association-Brigade 2506 and his term expires in 2022. He is a tireless fighter for Human rights and for the eventual removal of the communist dictatorship that has enslaved Cubans for the last 60 + years.

Letter to the European Court of Human Rights from the Committee to Assist Dissidents – Brigade 2506

After losing their appeal to the European Court of Human Rights, the Committee to Assist Dissidents, composed primarily of Brigade 2506 veterans, wrote a letter to The European Court of Human Rights Council of Europe condemning the arbitrary dismissal of their appeal. The original letter which is included below is in Spanish. The salient points are:

> The Court rejected out of hand the accusation of violation of human rights against the Castro Government and did not dispute the direct evidence of these crimes provided by individuals who were victims of these events.
>
> On the same day that the court ruled, Wilmar Villar Mendoza, a political prisoner in Castro's prisons died for expressing his beliefs in democracy and reform so the Cuban Government would follow the rule of law. He was just one of thousands of victims of the regime's police state.
>
> By arriving at this draconian and unjust decision, the tribunal is complicit with the Cuban Government, in perpetuating their dictatorial and abusive policies.

This is but another example of the double standard existing in international organizations regarding human right abuses.

CAD-2506
COMITE DE AYUDA A LA DISIDENCIA

Miami, 1 de mayo, 2012

European Court of Human Rights, Council of Europe
Attn: A.M. Mengual i Mallol, Letrada
67075 Strasbourg
Cedex, France

Ref.: Demanda No. 36858/09
Comité de Ayuda a la Disidencia – Brigada 2506 c. España

Sra. Letrada,

Después de analizar su escrito de enero 19 del corriente y de no encontrar una solución que nos permitiera continuar con nuestro empeño de encontrar una Corte que reconociera y diera curso a la demanda de referencia, hemos decidido enviar esta carta de protesta a su decisión.

Es vergonzoso ver con la indiferencia que el Tribunal Europeo de Derechos Humanos, representado en este caso por el juez único L.A. Sicilianos, ha tratado la muerte por asfixia de nueve víctimas del régimen dictatorial de los hermanos Castro. Esa indiferencia se hace aún mas incomprensible cuando se les ha presentado en nuestra demanda la evidencia que muestra de forma fehaciente que esas muertes constituyen un crimen y una clara violación a los derechos humanos de las victimas.

Es una ironía del destino que su carta de enero 19 fuera firmada el día en que muriera en las cárceles de Cuba, como resultado de una huelga de hambre, el Sr. Wilman Villar Mendoza, el cual estaba preso solo por expresar, de una forma pacífica, sus deseos de vivir en libertad y en un estado de derecho. El Sr. Villar Mendoza, al igual que las nueve víctimas de la demanda, son solo una pequeña parte de los miles de cubanos que han muerto por culpa de un régimen que ha perseguido brutalmente a sus opositores.

Con la decisión definitiva y de no recurso dictada por el Juez Sicilianos sobre nuestra demanda, creemos que el Tribunal Europeo de Derechos Humanos se ha hecho cómplice del régimen de La Habana y es moralmente partícipe de los crímenes que allí se cometen a diario. Solo nos queda esperar que la historia los juzgue debidamente.

Le agradeceríamos que enviara una copia de esta correspondencia al Juez L.A. Sicilianos.

Por el CAD-2506,

J.R. López de la Cruz
Director

P.O. Box 431406, South Miami, Florida 33243 U.S.A.   e-mail: cad2506@lacross.us

My Prayer

Lord I ask you
To give me the strength to be able to look at myself
In the mirror every day and say,
Today I did my personal best

Inspired by the Paratrooper's Prayer[105]

I bring this prayer to you, Lord
For You usually give
What one does not demand for one's self.

Give me Lord, what you have left over,
Give me what no one ever asks of you.

I don't ask you for rest or quiet
Whether of soul or body
I don't ask you for wealth,
Not for success, not even for health

That sort of thing you get asked for so much
That you can't have any of it left.

Give me Lord what you have left over,
Give me what no one wants from you.

---

[105] The Paratrooper's Prayer was written by Second Lieutenant André Louis Arthur Zirnheld, a paratrooper in the Free French Army. While serving with the British SAS deep behind enemy lines in Libya, he was killed in action on July 27, 1942. Found in his officer's notebook was a prayer entitled "The Paratrooper's Prayer" that he had written in Tunis in 1938. I find that many of my friends with similar backgrounds share these feelings.

Dark Nights in the Castle of the Prince

I want insecurity, strife, opportunity
The courage to make it happen
To do the right thing
And I want you to give me these things
Now and in the future.

So I can be sure of having them always,
Since I shall not always have the courage
To ask you for them.

Appendix 2:
Digital Images and Tables

Tables

Table 1. Sugar Production and Exports – Pre Revolution (1955-1958) and Post Revolution (1959 to1995) - Association for the Study of the Cuban Economy - https://www.ascecuba.org/ – November 30, 1995 (48)

Table 2. Brief Timeline of Cuban History (1492 to 1958) - Albert J Bolet - Teaching Aid (145)

Table 3. Consequences of the Failure to Depose Castro in 1961 - Albert J Bolet - Teaching Aid (151)

Images

Image 1. Wikipedia contributors. (2021, May 27). Castillo del Príncipe (La Habana). Photo: *Wikipedia, The Free Encyclopedia*. Retrieved 15:53, June 9, 2021, from https://en.wikipedia.org/ w/index.php?title=Castillo_del_Pr%C3%ADncipe_(Havana)&oldid=1025 327536. (14)

Image 2. My Brother and I - Bolet-Celorio Personal Collection: Photographs of Cuba (15)

Image 3. López-Calleja, A. J. (1949). Aeropuerto de Rancho Boyeros (Rancho Boyeros Airport). Bolet-Celorio Personal Collection: Photographs of Cuba (16)

Image 4. Wikipedia contributors. (2021, May 16). Claudio Brindis de Salas Garrido. In *Wikipedia, The Free Encyclopedia*. Retrieved 13:02, June 17, 2021, from https://en.wikipedia.org/w/ index.php?title=Claudio_Brindis_de_Salas_Garrido&oldid=1023513065 (22)

Image 5. Carnaval de La Habana - 1950 - http://memoriascubano.blogspocom/2014/03/carnavales-de-la-habana.html (23)

Image 6: Carnaval de La Habana - Carrozas - La carroza de Radio Progreso "La onda de la Alegría" con su reina Elvirita Delgado. En La Habana - Photo: Rogali (24)

Image 7: Comparsa Las Jardineras – Carnaval de la Habana - Ferguson, Erna (1946) Cuba. Alfred A. Knopp NY. (25)

Image 8. Playa de Varadero - Wikimedia Foundation. (2021, April 17). *Varadero*. Wikipedia. https://es.wikipedia.org/wiki/Varadero. (26)

Image 9. Colegio de la Salle, Miramar. Bolet-Celorio Personal Collection (27)

Image 10. My brother Armando, my sister Sylvita and I before a football game Bolet-Celorio Personal Collection (28)

Image 11: General Antonio Maceo y Grajales. commons.wikimedia.org/wiki/Category:Antonio_Maceo_Grajales (30)

Image 12: *Culver Summer School*. - Bolet-Celorio Personal Collection (33)

Image 13. Belen Track Team Bolet-Celorio Personal Collection (36)

Image 14. Castro and Kruschev hug - Castro and the Cold War https://www.pbs.org/wgbh/americanexperience/features/comandante-cold-war/ (42)

Image 15. The visit that rattled the State Department - https://nsarchive2.gwu.edu/NSAEBB/NSAEBB393/ - (49)

Image 16. Fusilamientos - Photograph by Andrew López - United Press International (52)

Image 17. Photo - Fontainebleau Hotel 1960 - City of Miami Beach miamibeachfl.gov (53)

Image 18. J Neville McArthur School of Engineering Building -Bolet-Celorio Personal Collection (55)

Image 19. US Ambassador Earl T Smith and Cuban President Fulgencio Batista - Photo: Latin American Studies http://www.latinamericanstudies.org/ (56)

Image 20. Multiple Planeloads of Refugees Arrived in Miami Every Day During the 1960's - Photo - Miami Herald (59)

Image 21. John Foster Dulles and Allen Dulles - Photo: Wall Street Journal Book Review - WSJ.com - https://www.wsj.com/ articles/SB10001424052702303471004579163723302927950 (60)

Image 22. Richard M Bissel - Deputy Director of Planning - US Central Intelligence Agency - Photo Wikipedia - https://en.wikipedia.org/wiki/Richard_M._Bissell_Jr. (62)

Image 23. Manuel Artime, José San Román, Antonio Maceo and Tony Varona in Guatemala Photo: Museo y Archivos de la Asociación de Veteranos de la Bahía de Cochinos - https://www.bayofpigsbrigade2506.com/ (65)

Image 24. Comandante Pedro Luis Diaz-Lanz -Photo: Latin American Studies http://www.latinamericanstudies.org/ (67)

Image 25. Some of the Cuban anticommunist forces that fought Castro and his Soviet advisors in the Escambray Mountains 1960-1965 - Photo: Latin American Studies http://www.latinamericanstudies.org/ (71)

Image26. Raúl and Margot Celorio - Photo: Bolet-Celorio Personal Collection (73)

Image 27. Celorio Family - Photo: Bolet-Celorio Personal Collection (75)

Image 28. Capture was followed by quick execution – no prisoners were taken - Photo: Latin American Studies - http://www.latinamericanstudies.org/ (80)

Image 29. Castro and Soviet Forces Executing Cuban Patriots in the Escambray Mountains 1961 Photo: Latin American Studies - http://www.latinamericanstudies.org/ (81)

Image 30 - Headline in Guatemalan newspaper Prensa Libre reporting on initial expulsion of 136 Catholic priests from Cuba who refused to pledge fealty to communist government - Copy of Front Page of Newspaper Prensa Libre 18 September 1961 (84)

Image 31. Flight Line of C-46 and C-54 aircraft used by the Brigade's Air Force at Base Trax, Retalhuleu, Guatemala - Photo: Museo y Archivos de la Asociación de Veteranos de la Bahía de Cochinos - https://www.bayofpigsbrigade2506.com/ (85)

Image 32. First Airborne Battalion Practice Jump – Quetzaltenango Guatemala Photo: Museo y Archivos de la Asociación de Veteranos de la Bahía de Cochinos - https://www.bayofpigsbrigade2506.com/ (87)

Image 33. Elements of First Airborne Battalion listening to a briefing by US CIA Advisors – April 16 1961 – Puerto Cabezas Air Base - Nicaragua https://www.bayofpigsbrigade2506.com/ (91)

Image 34. Admiral Arleigh Burke – Naval Chief of Staff - Naval History and Heritage Command - Photo: https://www.history.navy.mil/research/library/research-guides/modern-biographical-files-ndl/modern-bios-b/burke-arleigh.html (95)

Image 35. The modified invasion plan included landings at Playa Larga - Map from Museo y Archivos de la Asociación de Veteranos de la Bahía de Cochinos - https://www.bayofpigsbrigade2506.com/ (99)

Image 36. Satellite Image of the town of San Blas - our LZ - www.viamichelin.com/web/Maps/Map-San_Blas-_-Matanzas-Cuba (100)

Image 37. The Battalion of the Policía Nacional Revolucionaria attacked by Brigade's A-26 - Ferrer, E. B. (1993). Operation Puma: the Air Battle of the Bay of Pigs. (102)

Image 38. Sinking of the Houston Opposite Playa Larga - Archivos de la Asociación de Veteranos de la Bahía de Cochinos - https://www.bayofpigsbrigade2506.com/ (103)

Image 39. Lt. Rafael del Pino- of Castro's FAR - flew this T-33 jet. Photo: latin american studies.org. http://www.latinamericanstudies.org/baypigs-airforce.htm. (105)

Image 40 - Cuban T-34/85 tank staging near Playa Girón, April 1961. - Photo: Foreign Affairs Magazine - Council on Foreign Relations - https://www.foreignaffairs.com/ (106)

Image 41. Brigade Air Force A-26 on a bombing run over targets near Playa Larga - Illustration: Archivos de la Asociación de Veteranos de la Bahía de Cochinos - https://www.bayofpigsbrigade2506.com/ (110)

Image 42. VA-34's A4D-2 Skyhawks sortied from Essex (CVS 9) opposite Playa Girón during the Invasion Photo: United States Navy - CVS9 Air Group VA34 (111)

Image 43. Four Members of the Alabama Air National Guard killed flying missions over Girón - The four airmen killed. (n.d.). al.com. www.al.com/spotnews/2011/04/valor_and_tragedy_over_bay_of.html. (113)

Image 44. Alejandro del Valle – 1st Battalion (Airborne) Commander - Archivos de la Asociación de Veteranos de la Bahía de Cochinos - https://www.bayofpigsbrigade2506.com/ (114)

Image 45. Ciénaga de Zapata - Matanzas, Cuba - unknown photographer - Archivos de la Asociación de Veteranos de la Bahía de Cochinos - https://www.bayofpigsbri gade2506.com/ (115)

Image 46. Cuban majá snake – it is in the tree boa family - WikiPedia - https://en.wikipedia.org/wiki/Chilabothrus_angulifer (116)

Image 47. Brigade Prisoners Awaiting Transport to La Habana - Archivos de la Asociación de Veteranos de la Bahía de Cochinos - https://www.bayofpigsbri gade2506.com/ (118)

Image 48. Palacio de los Deportes – La Habana - Photo: Asociación de Veteranos de la Bahía de Cochinos - https://www.bayofpigsbri gade2506.com/ (125)

Image 49. President Reagan congratulates Erneido Oliva on his appointment to Major in the DC National Guard. He later advanced in rank to Major General. Photo: Asociación de Veteranos de la Bahía de Cochinos - https://www.bayofpigsbri gade2506.com/ (126)

Image 50. Hospital Naval 1962 – Habana del Este Cuba Photo: Asociación de Veteranos de la Bahía de Cochinos - https://www.bayof pigsbri gade2506.com/ (127)

Image 51: Castillo del Príncipe – Loma de Arostegui, La Habana Photo: Wikipedia, The Free Encyclopedia. (128)

Image 52. Entrance to Castillo del Príncipe - Photo: Wikipedia, The Free Encyclopedia. (132)

Image 53 Brigade Trial – Castillo del Príncipe – July 1962 - Photo: Asociación de Veteranos de la Bahía de Cochinos - https://www.bayofpigsbri gade2506.com/ (133)

Image 54: Entrance to the "Leoneras" - Photo: Asociación de Veteranos de la Bahía de Cochinos - https://www.bayofpigsbrigade 2506.com/ (135)

Image 55. The Author is reunited with his baby brother Peter at Dinner Key Auditorium Dec 25 1962 (L.A. Times Archives - AP Wire Photo) (139)

Image 56. President John F Kennedy receives Brigade Flag from Erneido Oliva - Photo: Asociación de Veteranos de la Bahía de Cochinos - https://www.bayofpigsbri gade2506.com/ (139)

Image 57. Margarita and I at our wedding – St Charles Catholic Church, Arlington VA - Photo: Bolet-Celorio Personal Collection (109)

Image 58. CV9 – USS Essex 1960's and CV21 USS Boxer - Photos: United States Navy (156)

Image 59. There were 6 Destroyers in the task force – shown: DDE-576 USS Murray - Photo: United States Navy (157)

Image 60. LSD – 25 USS San Marcos – Tank and Heavy Equipment Carrier - Photo: Asociación de Veteranos de la Bahía de Cochinos - https://www.bayofpigsbri gade2506.com/ (158)

Image 61. CIA Command and Control Ship - Barbara J - Photo: Asociación de Veteranos de la Bahía de Cochinos - https://www.bayof pigsbri gade2506.com/ (158)

Image 62. CIA – LSI Class Ship – Invasion Navy Flagship Blagar - Photo: Asociación de Veteranos de la Bahía de Cochinos - https://www.bayofpigsbri gade2506.com/ (159)

Image 63. Col Juan (Johnny) Lopez de la Cruz. Photo: Asociación de Veteranos de la Bahía de Cochinos - https://www.bayofpigsbrigade 2506.com/ (160)

BIBLIOGRAPHY

Boston : Little, Brown. (1991, January 1). *Guerrilla prince : the untold story of Fidel Castro : Geyer, Georgie Anne, 1935- : Free Download, Borrow, and Streaming.* Internet Archive. https://archive.org/details/guerrillaprinceu00geye.

Braun, H. (2003). *Assassination of Gaitan: Public life and urban violence in colombia.* Univ Of Wisconsin Pr.

Ferrer, E. B. (1993). *Operation Puma: the Air Battle of the Bay of Pigs.* International Aviation Consultants.

Foner, P. S. (1977). *Antonio Maceo the "Bronce Titan" of Cuba's Struggle for Independence.* Monthly Review Press.

"Jacobo Arbenz." (2021, January 23). https://www.britannica.com/biography/Jacobo-Arbenz.

Kline, H. F., Gavarito, C., Parsons, J. J., & Gilmore, R. L. (1999, July 26). Colombia - La Violencia, Dictatorship, and DemocraticRestoration. https://www.britannica.com/place/Colombia/La-Violencia-dictatorship-and-democratic-restoration.

Noyes, R. (2007, February 7). *Media Research Center Special Report.* Fidel's Flatterers: The U.S. Media's Decades of Cheering Castro's Communism. http://archive.mrc.org/SpecialReports/2007/castro/.

Ortega, L. M. y. (1936). *La isla de corcho; ensayo de economía cubana.* Maza, Caso y cía., imp.

Overall, M. (2016). *PBSuccess the Cia's covert operation to overthrow Guatemalan President Jacobo Arbenz, June-July 1954.* Helion & Company.

Pfeiffer, J. B. (1979, December). OFFICIAL HISTORY OF THE , BAY OF PIGS OPERATION VOLUME III EVOLUTION OF CIA's ANTI-CASTRO POLICIES, 1959-JANUARY 1961 (pages 1-203). Virginia. https://www.cia.gov/readingroom/docs/bop-vol3.pdf.

Pfeiffer, J. B. (1979, September). OFFICIAL HISTORY OF THE BAY OF PIGS OPERATION VOLUME II PARTICIPATION IN THE

CONDUCT OF FOREIGN POLICY. Virginia. https://www.cia.gov/readingroom/docs/bop-vol2-part1.pdf.

Pfeiffer, J. B. (1984, April 18). Official History of the Bay of Pigs Operation DRAFT Volume V CIA's Internal Investigation of the Bay of Pigs. Virginia. https://www.cia.gov/readingroom/docs/C01254908.pdf.

Pfeiffer, J. B. (1984, November 9). THE TAYLOR COMMITTEE INVESTIGATION OF THE BAY OF PIGS. Virginia. https://www.cia.gov/readingroom/docs/bop-vol4.pdf.

Pfeiffer, J. P. (1979, September). OFFICIAL HISTORY OF THE BAY OF PIGS OPERATION VOLUME I AIR OPERATIONS, MARCH 1960 - APRIL 1961. Virginia. https://www.cia.gov/readingroom/collection/bay-pigs-release.

Paratrooper's Prayer – La Priere du Para The American Society for the Defense of Tradition, Family and Property – https://www.tfp.org/the-paratroopers-prayer/

www.ingramcontent.com/pod-product-compliance
Lightning Source LLC
Chambersburg PA
CBHW030522080526
44586CB00011B/296